Pray Without Ceasing

Andrew J. Lamont-Turner

Published by Andrew J. Lamont-Turner, 2024.

PRAY WITHOUT CEASING

First edition. September 23, 2024.

ISBN: 979-8227876577

Written by Andrew J. Lamont-Turner.

Table of Contents

Pray without ceasing. In everything, give thanks, for this is the will of God in Christ Jesus toward you.
(1 Thessalonians 5:17-18)

Foreword

Most people consider prayer to be a means of communicating with God. As a result, irrespective of the spiritual label they wear, they pray more or less regularly. People believe in God instinctively. They must persuade themselves that God does not exist. People also pray instinctively. Christians are particularly interested in prayer. We think it is a means of communicating with the genuine God, who has shown Himself in love and has already spoken to us via His Word, the Bible. The two most important Christian figures, Jesus Christ and the Apostle Paul have the most to say about prayer in the Bible.

The amount of material accessible on prayer attests to the subject's popularity. Every month, new books about prayer arrive in bookshops worldwide. Some of these are scientific studies that look at prayer from a philosophical or psychological standpoint. Most of the publications in this category are devotional literature encouraging us to pray more. Few works, such as this one, deal with the problem from a religious standpoint. In other words, they strive to establish what the Bible says about prayer.

Except for the Song of Solomon, Obadiah, Haggai, and 2 John, prayers and allusions to prayer exist in sixty-two of the sixty-six books of the Bible. Because it is a collection of prayers, the Book of Psalms is in a class by itself.

The Bible portrays God as a being who has talked with us and asks us to do the same. We need to know what God has revealed about how we can and should speak with Him since He is our Creator and we are His finite created beings. By definition, Christians' connection with their heavenly Father is the most significant one that we have. As a result, we must understand how to interact with God acceptably and efficiently.

No text in the Bible defines prayer specifically. As a result, if we want a biblical meaning, we must examine the prayers and allusions to prayer in the Bible. Prayer is essentially a conversation with God. It is a way to convey our ideas and emotions to God.

Introduction

Talking to God is the most fundamental definition of prayer. Prayer is not meditation or passive thought; it directly communicates with God. The human soul's contact with the Lord who created the soul. Prayer is the fundamental means through which a believer in Jesus Christ communicates his feelings and wants to God and communion with God.

Prayer may be public or private, formal or informal, vocal or quiet. All prayer must be given in faith (James 1:6), in Jesus' name (John 16:23), and in the Holy Spirit's power (John 14:26; Romans 8:26).

In its complete New Testament meaning, Christian prayer is directed to God as Father, in the name of Christ as Mediator, and by the enabling power of the indwelling Spirit, according to the International Standard Bible Encyclopaedia ("Prayer" by J. C. Lambert).

Psalm 10:4 says that the wicked have no desire to pray, while God's children yearn to communicate with Him (Luke 11:1).

Seeking God's favour (Exodus 32:11), pouring out one's soul to the Lord (1 Samuel 1:15), crying out to heaven (2 Chronicles 32:20), drawing near to God (Psalm 73:28, KJV), and kneeling before the Father are all descriptions of prayer in the Bible (Ephesians 3:14).

Paul encourages us not to be concerned about anything; instead, we present our requests to God in prayer with thankfulness in every condition. God's peace will guard your hearts and minds in Christ Jesus (Philippians 4:6–7).

> *Don't be concerned about anything; instead,*
> *pray about everything.*

Everything? Yes, God desires that we communicate with Him about everything. How often should we pray? The biblical response is to "pray without ceasing" (1 Thessalonians 5:17). We should communicate with God throughout the day. Some people find the ACTS formula (discussed later) helpful in prayer; however, there is no unique formula for praying in the Bible. We should simply go ahead and do it. We can pray in any and all conditions. Prayer strengthens our connection with God and reveals our complete reliance on Him.

Prayer is a means for Christians to communicate with God. We pray to praise God, thank Him, and express our love for Him. We pray to be in His presence and inform Him about our lives. We pray to make requests, seek direction, and gain insight. God enjoys this interaction with His children just as much as we enjoy our interactions with our children. The core of prayer is fellowship with God. We lose sight of how easy prayer is meant to be all too frequently.

When we submit requests to God, we tell God where we are and what we want to see happen. We must acknowledge in our prayers that God is more prominent than we are and ultimately understands what is best in every scenario (Romans 11:33–36). God is good and invites us to put our confidence in Him. In prayer, we say, "Not my will, but your will be done." The key to receiving a response to prayer is to pray according to God's desire and in line with His Word. Prayer is not about pursuing our will but aligning ourselves more entirely with God's (1 John 5:14–15; James 4:3).

There are many instances of prayer in the Bible and several appeals to pray (see Luke 18:1, Romans 12:12, and Ephesians 6:18). God's home is to be a house of prayer (Mark 11:17). God's people are to be people of prayer:

But you, beloved, keep building up yourselves on your most holy faith, praying in the Holy Spirit. Keep yourselves in God's love, looking for the mercy of our Lord Jesus Christ to eternal life (Jude 1:20–21 WEB).

Purpose of prayer

Prayer is an essential component of the Christian life. It is how we converse with and worship the Lord. To comprehend the goal of prayer, it is necessary to first comprehend what prayer is not. Many false beliefs regarding prayer in the world and society, even among Christians, should be addressed first. Prayer is not the same as negotiating with God or placing demands on God.

Nor is prayer:
- merely requesting things from God
- a meditative, therapeutic exercise
- annoying God and consuming His time
- a means of exerting control over the Lord;
- a means of displaying one's spirituality in front of others.

Many individuals feel that prayer is just asking God for something. A suggestion is an aspect of prayer (Philippians 4:6), yet it is not the sole objective of prayer. Praying for our own and others' needs is necessary and reasonable, but there is much more to prayer. God is neither a genie who grants our every whim nor is He a weak God who can be swayed by our pleas.

The best method to understand the purpose of prayer is to look at Jesus' example during His earthly mission. Jesus prayed for Himself and others and for communion with the Father. John 17 is an excellent example of Jesus' use of prayer. He prays not just for the Father's glory but also for His followers and those who will believe in him (John 17:20). Another characteristic of Jesus' prayer habit that was stressed in His prayer in the Garden of Gethsemane was submission to the Father's will: "Yet not as I will, but as you will" (Matthew 26:39). Any request we make must be subject to God's will.

Prayer is a means of strengthening our connection with God. As He prayed to the Father during His earthly career, Jesus provided the example (Luke 6:12; Matthew 14:23). Relationships inherently strive to connect, and prayer is our communication with God. Others in the Bible who spent time praying include David, Hezekiah, and Paul.

Finally, the primary goal of prayer is worship. It is an act of worship when we pray to the Lord, acknowledging Him for who He is and what He has done. Several times, the Bible references prayer as an act of worship (see, for example, 2 Kings 19:15, John 12:28, and Romans 11:33–36). This aim should be reflected in how we pray. Our attention should be on who God is, not who we are.

Interestingly, the Lord's Prayer, which Jesus taught the disciples in Matthew 6:9–13, has these aspects. The first portion is dedicated to God's praise and adoration (Matthew 6:9). In contrast, the second part is dedicated to prayer for God's will to be done (Matthew 6:10). Following that, there is a plea for ourselves and others (Matthew 6:11–12) and a request for strength to face temptation (Matthew 6:13). This prayer was modelled by Jesus for His followers. It demonstrates all of the reasons for prayer with a significant worship emphasis.

Prayer is an essential component of the Christian life, and it is crucial to cultivate one's prayer practice. Prayer not only impacts our lives and the lives of others, but it is also a means of communicating with the Lord and growing in our relationship with Him. Prayer is fundamentally an act of adoration to the Lord. Because God's Word emphasises the power and purpose of prayer, it should not be overlooked.

Author Warren Wiersbe (2010:78) sums up the purpose of prayer:

"The immediate purpose of prayer is the accomplishing of God's will on earth; the ultimate purpose of prayer is the eternal glory of God."

God hears our prayers

Everything, even prayers, is heard by God. He is the Almighty. Nothing escapes His notice (Psalm 139:1–4). He rules over all He made (Isaiah 46:9–11). So the issue isn't whether God is aware of every request (He is) but if God is listening to our petitions to answer them.

God desires that we pray. He made prayer so that we may enjoy Him (Revelation 3:20), confess our sins (1 John 1:9), ask Him to supply our wants (Psalm 50:15) and align our wills with His (Jeremiah 29:11–12; Luke 22:42). One kind of prayer is sure to be answered. The prayer of repentance is described in Luke 18:13–14. When we come to the Lord in humble repentance, He eagerly justifies and forgives us.

It is crucial to remember that most of God's promises in Scripture were addressed to His people when contemplating prayer. Those promises were made to Israel and anyone who joined them in the Old Testament. Those promises were written to Jesus' disciples in the New Testament. It is a misapplication of Scripture to apply single passages to any context, even prayer. Even though the Lord knows and hears everything, He has specified particular situations in which He will not listen to our prayers:

1. God will not hear our prayers if we choose to continue in sin rather than repent and change. Though you hold out your hands in prayer, I conceal my eyes from you; even when you offer countless prayers, I am not listening, the Lord declares in Isaiah 1:15. Your hands are splattered with blood! If anybody turns a deaf ear to my counsel, even their prayers are filthy, says Proverbs 28:9.

For example, a young couple lives in sexual immorality together, yet they pray for God's blessing on their household.

2. God will not hear our prayers if we ask for things based on our selfish wants. "When you ask, you do not get," James 4:3 reads, "because you ask with improper intentions, so that you may spend what you receive on your pleasures."

For instance, a man is unsatisfied with his three-year-old Toyota and wishes for a brand-new Mercedes.

3. When what we seek is contrary to His will for us.

This is the boldness which we have toward him, that, if we ask anything according to his will, he listens to us (1 John 5:14 WEB).

For example, we pray passionately for a new job, but God's plan calls for us to remain where we are and be a testimony to our colleagues.

4. When we fail to ask with trust.

"Therefore I tell you, all things whatever you pray and ask for, believe that you have received them, and you shall have them." (Jesus says in Mark 11:24 WEB).

On the other hand, faith does not believe in something; it believes in Someone. Our faith is based on God's character and desire to bless and comfort us. When we pray, we must believe He hears us and will grant every request according to His plan (1 John 5:14–15).

For example, we may beg God to provide for a financial need while worrying and making untrue statements to our relatives and colleagues, such as "I'm certainly headed to the poorhouse." That money will never come to me."

God is holy, and He intends that we be holy as well (Leviticus 22:32; 1 Peter 1:16). When He realises that we, too, are pursuing purity, He is delighted to answer our prayers in ways that promote our spiritual progress.

"If you remain in me, and my words remain in you, you will ask whatever you desire, and it will be done for you" (Jesus states in John 15:7 WEB).

The key to prayer is to remain in Christ so that anything we ask comes from His heart (Psalm 37:4). Only then can we have faith that God hears our prayers and intends to answer them.

Function of Prayer

There is no secret recipe for praying. In its most basic form, Prayer is remaining in touch with God—talking to Him, spending time in His presence, and becoming close to Him. We show our admiration and appreciation to God via prayer, indicating our desires to Him, interceding for others, and learning more about His character and intentions for our lives.

Learning to pray is a natural element of developing our relationship with the Lord. We uncover the core of prayer as we create an active and ongoing relationship with God our Father via Jesus Christ, His Son, through the power of His indwelling Spirit.

Prayer is a distinctively human action; no other creatures have the opportunity to communicate with their Creator and Redeemer in this manner. However, prayer may be scary, particularly if you're new to the practice or have been trained to see prayer as a complicated, formal, or ritualised activity.

A saving connection with Jesus Christ is the cornerstone of effective prayer. Jesus instructed us to pray in His name (see John 16:23–24), under His authority, for what would honour and glorify God. We may confidently approach God's throne of grace because Jesus is our great high priest (Hebrews 4:14, 16).

Effective prayer must be given with trust (James 1:5–7). Jesus taught that part of praying in faith is perseverance in prayer and never giving up (Luke 18:1). Prayer is a social act. It should not be pushed but rather flow naturally from the heart since God knows what is in our hearts (Psalm 44:21; Luke 16:15; Acts 15:8; Romans 8:27).

Prayer stems from God's love for us. As children of a loving Father, we may rely on God to provide for our needs (Isaiah 64:8–9; Psalm 103:13–14).

If we really want to understand how prayer works, we should examine the prayer life of Jesus Christ. Jesus, more than anybody else, had a close personal relationship with God the Father. As a result, He is the ideal model for us to follow. Jesus taught His disciples the following about prayer (discussed further in Jesus' teaching on prayer):

"When you pray, you shall not be as the hypocrites, for they love to stand and pray in the synagogues and in the corners of the streets, that they may be seen by men. Most certainly, I tell you, they have received their reward. But you, when you pray, enter into your inner room, and having shut your door, pray to your Father who is in secret, and your Father who sees in secret will reward you openly. Don't use vain repetitions in praying, as the Gentiles do, for they think they will be heard for their much speaking. Therefore, don't be like them, for your Father knows what you need before you ask him (Matthew 6:5-8 WEB).

Jesus emphasised the need for genuine, passionate prayer based on a love connection with God the Father.

Pastor and author Andrew Murray (1895:6) defined appropriate prayer:

As to the glory of God, in complete submission to His will, in full confidence of faith, in the name of Jesus, and with a persistence that, if necessary, refuses to be denied.

We've just touched the surface of how prayer works thus far. Much more is spoken about in the Bible. However, the ultimate conclusion is that prayer works via the believer's continual connection with the living God. Those who follow Christ have the rare opportunity to spend their lives learning more and more about prayer via a loving connection with their heavenly Father.

God answers prayers

God promises to provide us what we ask for if we ask for things in conformity with His desire for our life (1 John 5:14–15). However, we may not always agree with the solution.

We pray for various reasons, some good, some negative, and others completely meaningless. But God hears all of our prayers, no matter what we ask (Matthew 7:7). He does not turn His back on His children (Luke 18:1–8). He has promised to listen and answer when we speak to Him (Matthew 6:6; Romans 8:26–27). His response may be anything like "yes," "no," or "wait, not now."

Remember that prayer is not a mechanism for getting God to do what we desire. Our prayers should be directed toward things that honour and praise God and reflect what the Bible plainly shows to be God's desire (Luke 11:2). If we pray for anything that dishonours God or is contrary to His desire for us, He is unlikely to grant our request. God's knowledge vastly outweighs ours, and we must believe that His answers to our prayers are the most satisfactory solutions available.

When God says "yes."

Hannah prays to God for a child in the first two chapters of 1 Samuel. She had been unable to conceive, which was considered a mark of shame for a woman in biblical times. Hannah prayed fiercely—so frantically, in fact, that a priest who observed her praying mistook her for intoxicated. But God heard Hannah and enabled her to have a child.

"Whatever you ask in my name, I will accomplish," Jesus responded, "so that the Father may be exalted in the Son" (John 14:13). If you have explicitly asked for something. God has given it to you. You may be confident that it is His will. Nothing occurs unless God allows it to happen (Romans 8:28).

When God says "no."

In John 11, Mary and Martha pleaded with Jesus to cure their sick brother, but Jesus let Lazarus die. Why did He say "no" to these bereaved ladies who adored Him? Because He had bigger plans for Lazarus, which no one could have predicted.

"No" is one of the most challenging responses we may hear. But, once again, it is critical to remember that God is all-knowing and mindful of the universe's history. He knows every possible result and decision in every possible event, whilst we are not. He sees the "vast picture," whereas we just perceive a sliver of a brushstroke.

"Trust in the LORD with all your heart, and do not depend on your understanding" (Proverbs 3:5 WEB).

When we get a "no," we must accept that whatever we requested was not God's will.

When God says, "wait."

Hearing "wait" might be more complex than hearing "no" since it requires us to be patient (Romans 8:25). While it is tough to wait, we may be happy that God is in control and believe that His time will be perfect (Romans 12:12; Psalm 37:7—9).

God just wants the best for you. He does not want you to suffer in vain. "For I know the plans I have toward you, declares the Lord, plans for welfare and not for you, to give you a future and a hope," Jeremiah 29:11 reads. Be patient, and remember that He is your loving Father (Psalm 46:10).

As you present your requests to God, remember Philippians 4:6 (WEB):

"Do not be worried about anything, but in everything, via prayer and supplication with thanksgiving, let your requests be made known to God."

Then, when God replies, be ready to accept His counsel, whether or not you agree with it.

Pray without Ceasing

Paul's injunction in 1 Thessalonians 5:17 to "pray without ceasing" may seem confusing. This does not mean that we should spend the entire day with our heads bowed and our eyes shut. Paul alludes to a continual condition of God-consciousness, surrendering to God rather than perpetual speaking. We should realise that God is present and actively involved in our actions and thoughts every waking minute.

When our minds stray to despair, anxiety, discouragement, or fury, we must deliberately and immediately change every thought into prayer and thankfulness. Paul urges us in the letter to the Philippians to submit our desires to God in everything, through prayer and petition, with thankfulness (Philippians 4:6). He told the Colossian Christians to devote themselves to prayer. In contrast, attentive and thankful (Colossians 4:2). Paul urged the Ephesian Christians to see prayer as an instrument to be utilised in spiritual battles (Ephesians 6:18). Prayer must be our first response to each unpleasant event, worrying idea, or undesirable activity God assigns us to complete throughout the day. We depend on ourselves and more on God's grace when we don't pray. At its root, unending prayer is a condition of perpetual dependence on and communication with the Father.

For Christians, prayer must be as essential as it gets. You shouldn't have to concentrate on breathing because the environment exerts pressure on your lungs and forces you to. Holding your breath is thus more challenging than breathing. Similarly, when adopted into God's family, we enter a spiritual world in which God's existence and grace exert pressure or affect our lives. Prayer is a natural response to such stress. Christians have all entered the sacred atmosphere to keep breathing prayer.

Regrettably, many Christians suppress their spiritual breathing for long periods, assuming that brief interactions with God are sufficient to keep them alive. However, such a limit on their spiritual intake stems from evil desires. To succeed, a believer must be continually in God's presence, breathing in His truths.

It is easier for Christians to feel confident when they assume rather than rely on God's favour. Too many Christians are content with physical benefits and slightly yearning for spiritual ones. When programmes, techniques, and money yield excellent outcomes, they conflate human accomplishment with heavenly favour. When this occurs, there will be no deep desire for God or yearning for His assistance. Continuous, persistent, and unceasing prayer is integral to Christian existence and stems from humility and reliance on God.

Jesus' teaching on prayer

In some ways, the notion of prayer in the Old Testament ends with the end of the Old Testament. In another sense, it extends into Christ's life since He lived under the rules that controlled Israel. As it was conducted during Jesus' time, Prayer was merely a continuation of Old Testament traditions. Thus, prayer during the messianic time resembles what prevailed in Israel under Mosaic law roughly 400 years after returning from exile.

This epoch has seen the most significant breakthroughs in the gradual revelation of prayer than any other. Jesus' teaching on prayer and His personal prayer practice shed fresh light on the issue. Jesus spoke more about prayer than any other biblical figure. We will look at what Jesus taught about prayer by categorising it according to how He conveyed it. We will examine His personal example first, then His direct instructions on prayer, and lastly, His indirect teachings on this topic. Our primary source of knowledge is the Gospels.

Many of Jesus' prayers are not recorded in the Gospels. In fact, if we read them all at once, we could probably finish in under 10 minutes. However, the Gospel authors characterised Jesus as a guy who spent much time praying. Perhaps we don't have many of His prayers because what He taught and exhibited was more significant than the words He said to His Father. Jesus was neither a recluse nor a hermit. He did not withdraw from society but instead led an active and busy life in Israel. Prayer was a natural part of his life, with which current Christians can ultimately connect.

Jesus made it a practice to pray before significant events in His life. His baptism was among these events, which marked the beginning of His public ministry (Luke 3:21). He prayed before His disciples were chosen (Luke 6:12-13), before His transfiguration (Luke 9:29), and before His crucifixion (Luke 22:39-46; John 17; cf. Heb. 5:7).

The example of Jesus praying in Gethsemane is noteworthy (Luke 22:3946). As He prepared for His arrest, trials, and execution, Jesus prayed to His Father. He did so, in part, to avoid succumbing to temptation (Luke 22:46).

They fell asleep because the disciples did not see their desperate need for God's assistance. But Jesus foresaw confrontation and prayed to prepare for it.

It's also vital to remember what He prayed in Gethsemane. As a man, He strived to accomplish God's desire.

"Father, if you are willing, take this cup from me; but not my will, but yours be done," he pleaded (Luke 22:42 (WEB).

There are various signs in the Gospels and elsewhere in the New Testament that when Jesus became a man, He accepted humanity's limitations. He preserved God's nature and assumed man's nature, complete with human limitations. He, for example, limited His human presence to a single spot at a time. He said He did not know some things because He decided to restrict His omniscience during His incarnation (Matthew 24:36; see also Philippians 2:6-7). As a result, when Jesus prayed, He prayed as a man. Luke's Gospel, which emphasises Jesus' humanity, has the most information on Jesus' prayer life of any Gospel.

In Gethsemane, Jesus made a plea to His Father. He requested that the cup be removed from Jesus if it was the Father's wish. The cup is a well-known Old Testament symbol of divine judgement. The prophets predicted that God would pour out the cup of His anger on many of Israel's neighbours. If it was God's will, Jesus asked to be spared from bearing the penalty for mankind's crimes. On the other hand, He submerged one desire beneath another that was more essential to Him. He mostly prayed for God's will to be done.

This prayer is beneficial to follow since we frequently do not know God's plan. Is it the will of God for Aunt Sally to recover from her illness? Is it God's plan for us to fly to San Diego on Thursday? Jesus' prayer pattern invites us to convey our preferences to God while submitting them to God's will. Disciples of Jesus Christ should seek God's will above everything else, even our preferences.

That priority was shown by Jesus in the way He prayed in Gethsemane, and we should follow in His footsteps. When we know God's will, we may confidently pray for it. When unsure, we should pray according to His will, as Jesus did here.

It is also worth noting that Jesus prayed for others. He prayed for people like Peter (Luke 22:32), the soldiers around His crucifixion (Luke 23:34; see also Isaiah. 53:1), and His present and future disciples (John 17:6-26). His intercessory ministry is still active today (Romans 8:34; Hebrews 7:25). He begs from the heavens for His own.

There are three primary sources of Jesus' teaching on prayer in the Gospels, plus incidental teachings. The four primary sources are the Lord's Prayer, Jesus' parables, His Upper Room Discourse, and His high priestly prayer.

Teaching on the Lord's Prayer

On two distinct occasions, Jesus taught what we now call the Lord's Prayer. It is the "Lord's Prayer" in that it originated from Him rather than that He prayed it. The account in Matthew's Gospel takes place during the Sermon on the Mount (Matthew 6:9-13). Jesus taught His followers how to live in this discourse. In answer to a query from His followers, after He had completed praying privately, Jesus restated His teaching on prayer, with slight changes (Luke 11:2-4). In both instances, He instructed disciples (Matthew 5:1; Luke 11:1), individuals who wanted to learn from Him as an authoritative teacher. Some may have already thought He was the God-man, while others, like Judas Iscariot, had not. As a result, His teaching was not confined to believers alone, but it was obviously meant for those who did and would believe in Him. The fact that this concept is repeated throughout Scripture attests to its value.

Jesus delivered His message in two distinct ways. In the Sermon on the Mount, He instructed His disciples to pray "in this manner" (Matthew 6:9), yet on occasion reported by Luke, He said, "When you pray, say..." As a model prayer, Jesus meant what He taught as a model for His followers' prayers and as a prayer that they may repeat.

He did not confine their prayers to these phrases but provided them with prayer advice.

What Jesus said first was perhaps the most essential item He taught in the Lord's Prayer. When His followers come to Him in prayer, Jesus instructs them to think of God as their heavenly Father. As I previously said, how a person believes in God influences how they pray.

It was novel when Jesus initially established the concept of God as the personal Father of individual Christians. The Old Testament refers to God as the collective Father of the country of Israel. Still, it never referred to Him as the Father of individual Israelites. There is no evidence that the rabbis of Jesus' day had this understanding of God.

As a result, this concept most likely astounded Jesus' audience. To address God as one's Father certainly sounded too intimate. But Jesus taught us to think of God as a loving Father in heaven when we approach Him in prayer. He lacks the flaws that characterise worldly dads. He is the ultimate parent in heaven and is what every father should be.

When we pray, we might imagine God in a variety of ways. After all, he is the Sovereign King of the Universe, the Almighty God, the Eternal God, the Covenant Keeper, the Victorious Warrior, and so on. It is undoubtedly reasonable to conceive of God in all these positions since He has shown Himself in numerous ways. However, when Jesus' followers pray to God, it is most natural and valuable for us to conceive of Him as our heavenly Father. Why? Because it will influence how and what we pray to some degree. It should encourage us to be open and honest with God.

On the other hand, since He is God, our heavenly Father, we must revere Him (cf. Ecclesiastes 5:2). The father in the family deserved considerable respect and adoration from the Oriental perspective, distinctive of Jesus' culture. A good son modelled his life on his father's and followed in his father's footsteps. Our prayer troubles will be alleviated if we think of God as our heavenly Father.

Jesus next instructed His followers on how to pray for six different things. He, or Luke, simplified His previous teaching in the Luke report. The first three requests address God's needs, while the final three address the disciples' needs. This implies that our initial priority in prayer should be what is most essential to God, followed by what we need. A committed son and disciple should prioritise his Father's interests. Inadvertently, this arrangement reveals something about the aim of prayer. It is not mainly for our benefit but to enhance God's honour and design.

The first petition asks that God's name be sanctified. God's name encapsulates all about Him and is synonymous with His renown. When we pray for this, we ask that everyone respect God with reverence, including ourselves. Holy signifies are distinct, particularly from sinful people. God's purity is unrivalled. His affection is unadulterated. His statements are sincere. His intentions are good. His personality is unblemished. He is a man of total honesty. When we pray for His name to be hallowed, we pray that others recognise Him for who He is. One of our responsibilities as His followers is representing Him to others unfamiliar with Him. Jesus stated here that one of our key goals should be for others to come to know Him for who He really is. That is essential for Him to be glorified and for people to be blessed.

Next, Jesus instructed us to pray for the arrival of God's kingdom. God revealed a great deal about His eventual kingdom in the Old Testament. He vowed that it would happen one day and that a Davidic descendant would govern the nations with an iron shepherd's rod.

The iron rod represented a shepherd's perfect tool (Psalm 2). So when we pray the second petition, we are not praying that the kingdom will come, but rather that it will not. It will arrive, as God has promised. We are hoping it will arrive shortly. We are expressing our desire to establish God's authority, which will result in the dismissal of our Savior and the rebalancing of the balances of justice. John the Baptist and Jesus appeared, proclaiming that the promised kingdom of the Old Testament had arrived. If the Israelites had embraced Jesus as their Messiah when He taught this prayer, it might have arrived very soon. They did not do so. As a result, the kingdom is still in the future. As John the Baptist and Jesus did, Jesus' followers should anticipate and pray for its arrival. The arrival of that kingdom will be the most beautiful thing this earth has ever seen. As a result, we can understand why Jesus advised us to put it at the forefront of our thoughts and prayers.

The third petition, which Jesus left out from his recital of this teaching in Luke, addresses one feature of the first. When God's kingdom arrives, His will on earth will be done as in heaven. Still, we should not be satisfied just sitting back and waiting for the kingdom to arrive. As we await the kingdom's arrival, we should prioritise fulfilling God's will. We should not only do God's will ourselves, but we should also endeavour to bring it into our world right now.

Praying for it reminds us that it is only possible if God grants us grace and assistance.

God's will is not manifested just via law or social activity. It must be brought about by God. This is why we must prioritise fulfilling God's will in the here and now in our prayers.

The last three requests address the primary personal needs of the disciples.

First, we must pray to God for our daily food. This prayer reminds us that God provides for all of life's requirements. Bread often represents fundamental requirements in the Bible, as it does in contemporary symbology. When discussing bread as the bread of life, we talk about more than simply flour kneaded and baked into loaves. We're using bread metaphorically to symbolise life's essentials (cf. Matthew 4:4). We hope that God will supply us with the resources to serve Him as His disciples.

Furthermore, Jesus reminded us that we need these things daily. We must recognise that we live from hand to mouth because He gives us these things. We rely on Him for all we need daily and must express our reliance on Him in prayer. We need His sustenance now and every day. We rely on Him to provide for our needs now and every day.

Some Christians argue that requesting bodily necessities demonstrates a lack of confidence in God's love, faithfulness, and capacity to give. Making these requests seems to them to demonstrate a lack of faith rather than confidence in God. However, Jesus Christ instructed us to pray to God for what we need to carry out His will. Indeed, God is loving, reliable, and capable of providing without asking. Nonetheless, He has instructed us to seek Him for what we need. We would lose sight of the fact that these things come from Him and that we rely on Him for them if we never asked Him for them.

Praying for what we need is a practice of reliance. It assists us in keeping ourselves and God in the proper perspective. He is the basis of all good gifts (James 1:17), and we rely entirely on Him to supply our needs (John 15:5).

Because we sin regularly, we must seek God's forgiveness and supply. Debts are what we owe to others, people, and God for offending them (Matthew 6:11). Sins are all our transgressions against God and others. In Luke 11:4, Jesus or Luke used the broad term for sins. We forgive individuals who owe us as proof that we recognise our need for forgiveness. In Matthew 6:14-15, Jesus emphasised the significance of forgiving others to receive heavenly forgiveness. Before we may experience a clear vertical connection with our heavenly Father, we must rectify our horizontal relationships.

This doctrine is not contradicted by God's promises to forgive the sins of those who believe in His Son in the past, present, and future (Romans 8:1). God once and for all forgives the shame of our transgressions. He will never judge us for our transgressions. However, as God's forgiven sons, we may offend God with our sins, impacting our daily relationship. As a result, we must confess our sins (1 John 1:9), not to ensure our salvation but to reestablish our connection with God. Confession guarantees familial forgiveness, while justification secures forensic or legal forgiveness. When we sin, God does not exclude us from His family, yet our connection with Him suffers, so we must confess our faults as believing disciples.

At first, the sixth and final petition may seem to include a conflict in biblical revelation. According to James (James 1:13), God does not tempt anybody, yet Jesus instructed us to pray that He would not tempt us. The answer seems to be that Jesus used another form of speech, this time litotes. Litotes are figures of speech that express a positive concept using their inverse. For example, "that's no big problem" signifies "that's a little issue;" it is inconsequential. "Do not lead us into temptation" literally means "Do not lead us into temptation." God does not tempt anybody, yet He enables us to be tempted by the world, the flesh, and the devil (Job 1—2; 1 John 2:15-17; Romans 7:18-24; 1 Peter 5:8). By praying this prayer, we convey our sincere desire for God's protection from any temptation that may come our way. It supplicates asking God to enable us to be tempted as little as possible. It expresses our need for God's assistance in avoiding and coping with temptation.

The flip side of the coin, which Luke did not report, is included in Jesus' teaching in Matthew. We want deliverance from evil or wicked; either translation is acceptable. Rather than succumbing to temptation, we pray for freedom from it and the evil it spawns and leads to.

In Matthew's last doxology, God is forever given dominion, power, and glory. There is substantial debate whether this sentence was included in the original autograph of Matthew's Gospel or whether it was added later by a scribe. I'd instead include it. In any instance, it reflects an emotion that ought to be repeated.

The first three pleas address the individual, the programme, and God's power.

For His disciple sons, His interests should come first. The second three are about His sustenance, forgiveness, and protection. These requests describe our most fundamental requirements.

In addition, Jesus taught His followers three stories on prayer.

Teaching about God's Desire to Bless

When Jesus reiterated His teaching in the Lord's Prayer, He followed it up with a parable and more instruction (Luke 11:5-13). The narrative has been dubbed "the parable of the persistent friend." Yet, the proper focus is on God's graciousness, not the friend's perseverance. The tale is found in Luke 11:5-8, and the Lord's teaching on prayer continues until verse 13.

The parable's lesson is that perseverance triumphs when friendship fails. Even though the buddy would not get up and offer his neighbour what he desired since he was his friend, his perseverance convinced him to accept his request (Luke 11:8). Suppose we accepted the storey on its own. In that case, we may infer that Jesus' argument was that we can gain things from God via prayer if we persevere in asking Him for things He would not give us if we did not persist. This is correct; another tale emphasises the need for prayerful perseverance (Luke 18:1-8). However, the goal of this parable is different. It only sets the setting for the subsequent instruction. In verses 9-13, we learn that although perseverance is necessary, we must also acknowledge something more significant as we pray. We must realise that our heavenly Father's heart differs from the heart of the friend who eventually agreed to his neighbour's plea in the parable. Jesus taught here by comparing individuals and their mindsets as He often did.

He specifically compared the friend's hesitancy with the Father's willingness.

Verse 9 encourages Jesus' followers to continue asking our heavenly Father, seeking what we need from Him and knocking on heaven's door to acquire our necessities (cf. vv. 3-4). The process of prayer is from the least desperate to the most desperate. In each circumstance, regardless of how deeply we may feel the need for God's provision, Jesus guaranteed that God will grant us everything we ask for. He does not just give to those who knock often and loudly. He also provides to those who continue to ask. This text focuses on God's readiness to give us what we need, not the value of our perseverance in prayer.

In verse 10, Jesus reiterated this argument, most likely because it is difficult to accept.

In the Lord's Prayer context, "everyone" refers to disciples who pray to God for things that glorify Him, promote His will, and allow them to serve Him. This scripture is a tremendous motivator for disturbing God with these demands. The buddy who arrived at midnight and knocked on his neighbour's door did not get a warm welcome. In contrast, God will gladly welcome anybody who comes to Him and asks for the things Jesus instructed the disciples to pray for in the Lord's Prayer (vv. 2-4). There is no such thing as a terrible moment to make such a request. God does not slumber at night; He is always awake and ready to assist. His other tasks do not prevent Him from replying to us when we ask; He is glad to assist. We can rely on Him to provide us with everything we need!

In verses 11 and 12, Jesus demonstrated how ready and eager God is to offer these incredible things to those who seek Him. When their sons beg for items they need, good dads should not give them things that may hurt them. In Jesus' day, fish and eggs were commonplace consumables everyone ate. What parent would replace a snake or a scorpion resembling a fish and an egg for something that would disappoint and even imperil his son?

In verse 13, Jesus brought this lecture to a close. If human dads would not offer their kids a poor replacement for what they need, how much more will the heavenly Father only give His sons what is best for them?

When Jesus offered this teaching, the Holy Spirit was God's most acceptable gift to humanity. He only provided it sparingly in the Old Testament; few Christians had the indwelling Spirit (cf. John 14:17). Being enabled by God's Spirit was the most significant benefit a Jew could have in Jesus' day. In this instance, Jesus utilised the Holy Spirit to illustrate God's most acceptable gift to one of His children. We do not need to seek God for His Spirit in our day, for the Holy Spirit indwells every believer (Romans 8:9). It was proper for Peter, James, and John to beg for the Spirit before Pentecost. Still, we do not need to do so. We don't need more of Him since we already have Him in His fullness; He only needs complete dominion over us (Romans 6:13; 12:1-2; Galatians 5:16).

This revelation should persuade every follower of Jesus Christ that when we approach our heavenly Father in prayer and ask for the things Jesus instructed us to pray for, He will provide them. We may have to keep asking, seeking, and knocking for a while, but God will always provide for our needs. We can rely on this because of the nature of our God. As the parable's neighbour was, he is more than merely an excellent buddy. He is our heavenly Father. He doesn't even act like a friendly, worldly parent. He acts in the manner of a flawless heavenly Father.

This prayer instruction is essential for Jesus Christ's followers, those called into God's family and sent forth on a divine mission (Matthew 28:19-20). It assures us that God will supply all we need to fulfil the calling He has kindly given us (Matthew 28:19-20).

Jesus Encourages to Pray

In the previous discourse, Jesus warned His followers that they may have to wait a while before God granted their prayer request. Because answers to prayer are not always instantaneous, we might get disheartened and question whether they will ever arrive. Jesus used the tale in Luke 18:1-8 to urge His followers to constantly pray and not give up (v. 1).

Jesus compared our heavenly Father with a friend and an earthly father (Luke 11:5-8; Luke 11:11-12). He compared the heavenly Judge with an earthly judge in this one. Previously, the focus was on giving from a place of love.

It is on the handing out of justice here.

The judge in the tale was everything a judge in Israel should not be.

He did not fear God and showed no regard for those needing justice. He was insensitive to the cries of a widow who, in Jesus' day, would have been without an advocate and impoverished, and he was self-centred. The only reason he ultimately caved into her incessant requests was that she wore him down. She irritated him to no end.

In verse 7, Jesus contrasted God, the just Judge, with this corrupt judge. This evil judge had limited authority in one city, but God is the Judge of all people.

Because he was evil, the judge in the parable dealt justice unwillingly. Still, God will rule fairly because He is a just Judge. The evil judge delivered justice to someone he had no care for, but God will deliver justice to those He has chosen as His children. If a nameless widow's continuous appeals moved this cruel judge, how much more would God's elect's persistent prayers move Him? Suppose the evil judge reacted pretty swiftly due to the widow's tenacity. How much faster will God listen to His elect's persistent cries?

Jesus closed His lecture by promising His students that God will bring them justice as soon as possible (v. 8). When we go out into the world as Christ's ambassadors, we regularly face unfair treatment from the non-elect. We pray to God to grant us justice and prevent the adversary from triumphing over us. Jesus prophesied that God will swiftly deliver justice to His chosen people.

But what about the unjustly killed Christian martyrs? God does not seem to have delivered justice to them quickly. The explanation is most likely found in how we understand the relative phrase "quickly." This prayer instruction is set in the perspective of the Lord's return at the end of the age (Luke 17:37; 18:8b). In Jesus' future revelations, one lifetime is not very lengthy. Rapidly, it does not always imply during one's lifetime.

"With the Lord, one day is as a thousand years, and a thousand years as one day" (2 Pet. 3:8 WEB).

The Lord's coming is mentioned again after verse 8. (cf. Luke 17:37). There will be few Christians left on the planet when He arrives, and there will be little faith. Our faith, though, may be shown in our prayers. As emphasised by Jesus in this tale, persistence in prayer indicates confidence in God. As the end times approach, we must continue to pray steadfastly and not lose heart (v. 1), regardless of the injustice we may face. As the world's end approaches, Jesus encourages His followers to pray faithfully. God is a fair and loving Judge who will swiftly deliver justice to His poor and needy chosen, even if that justice comes after we die.

Teaching about Humility

In Luke's Gospel, another tale follows what we discussed (Luke 18:9-14). The second one came after the first in chronological order. They are also related since they both deal with prayer. This tale of the Pharisee and the Tax Collector reminds us to humble ourselves when approaching God, particularly in prayer.

The Pharisee was typical in his pride in himself and his noble actions. Because of his activities, he felt that God and others would see him favourably. The publican, or tax collector, did not mention himself as a cause for God to hear and answer his prayer. He just threw himself on God's mercy, believing in God for forgiveness rather than himself. Jesus taught that God appreciates the tax collector's attitude, not the Pharisees. Those who believe in God's kindness, rather than those who proclaim themselves righteous, are justified and declared righteous by God.

When we pray, we must have the same mentality as Jesus' followers. We must place ourselves at God's mercy and not demand that He recognise us due to our actions. By humbling ourselves, we position ourselves for God to glorify us (cf. James 4:10; 1 Peter 5:6). The humble Christian will pray; the prideful Christian will not. It is worth noting that the Pharisees made no supplication to God. Prayer for him was a method for displaying his religious conduct, not a way for God to heal him. This parable teaches the importance of the right attitude in prayer, an attitude of dependence.

Upper Room Discourse

Jesus met His disciples in an upper room just before His betrayal, imprisonment, and crucifixion to prepare them for what was coming. Jesus taught them many things as they sat around a table late that night (John 14—16). All of what He said prepared them for the day He would be gone in heaven, and they would be carrying out His job for them on Earth. He taught them about prayer as part of what He taught them.

Jesus taught the disciples to pray to their heavenly Father on the authority of Jesus Christ Himself while He was away. When they prayed "in my name," God would grant them what they asked for, Jesus stated (John 14:13, 14; 15:16; 16:23, 24). The Apostle John recognised the significance of praying in Jesus' name and articulated what Jesus meant in his first letter (1 John 5:14-15).

Requesting in Jesus' name entails asking and following God's desire. It asks for things we know are God's will or things that are subject to God's will (cf. Luke 22:42). Praying in Jesus' name does not imply concluding our prayers with "... in Jesus' name, amen." It entails prayer based on the person and work of Jesus Christ.

His name, not yours, makes all the difference. Jesus has made the Father's resources accessible to us as disciples and the circumstances under which we might tap into His boundless riches. If His disciples begged Him for anything that was per God's will, Jesus vowed to give it to them. The objective of the request and response is for the Father to be glorified (John 14:13). For emphasis, Jesus reaffirmed the promise multiple times (John 14:14; 15:16; 16:23, 24). The disciples would experience lasting fruit (John 15:16) and fullness of delight as a consequence (John 16:24).

The extra promise in John 15:7 ensures that devoted followers get everything they ask for in prayer. The term "abide" is crucial to this pledge. This phrase was used by Jesus and John to refer to disciples who believed in Jesus and lived in friendship with Him (cf. 1 John 1:1-4). Not all Christian aspirations are in sync with God's. Sometimes, we ask for things so that we may devour them to satisfy our own desires, not so that we can carry out God's purpose (James 4:3). However when we are walking with the Lord and desiring to fulfil His will, we will pray for what is following His will and for His glory. Those are the demands He promised to fulfil.

Jesus mentioned prayer three times in this discourse: at the start, middle, and conclusion. This demonstrates the significance of prayer to the disciples' ministry in the inter-advent era. Jesus mentioned the disciples' prayers to Him and the Father. Either individual has the right to be addressed in prayer. However, since the Son, in the Trinity, praises the Father, it is more acceptable to direct our petitions to the Father in the name of the Son and with the enabling of the Spirit.

Jesus' High Priestly Prayer

Jesus' prayer in John 17 is the longest recorded by the Gospel evangelists. It is significant in the Fourth Gospel. Prayers often accompanied farewell addresses delivered by notable persons under divine inspiration in the Old Testament (cf. Genesis 49; Deuteronomy 32—33). This one came at the end of Jesus' last Upper Room Discourse (John 14—16). The prayer's topic is God's glory and the disciples' welfare. The disciples' mission was critical in Jesus' mind; this is what Jesus prayed for. This prayer foreshadows His current intercessory role. According to John 18:1, Jesus most likely recited this prayer before entering Gethsemane, either in the upper chamber or near Jerusalem.

Jesus made requests for Himself in the first five lines. His deepest desire was to praise His Father. That should be the motivating motivation of His followers as well. That desire led to Jesus' petition here and should also lead to our prayers. Only as a means to the aim of the Father's ultimate glory did Jesus ask for His own glorification.

The glory of Jesus was contingent on the well-being of those whom the Father had entrusted to Him, His followers. As a result, Jesus also prayed for them (vv. 6-19). The length of this passage implies that Jesus' care for His followers outweighed His concern for Himself (cf. Luke 6:12; John 6:15; Luke 22:32; Romans 8:34; Hebrews 7:25). It was God's sustaining force, not the disciples' strength, that gave Jesus confidence as He prayed for them. Jesus's wishes were founded on the notion that God had selected the disciples from the world and belonged to God. He prayed especially for those who had placed their trust in Him. They had a particular bond with Him. Because Jesus would leave them, they required special assistance from the Father. Then Jesus prayed for their protection and sanctification (vv. 11b-16; vv. 17-19). These worries are indeed still present in Jesus' prayers for His own.

The prayer concludes with Jesus' prayers for future Christians (vv. 20-26). These people would believe in Him due to what the first generation of disciples observed. He asked for their unity (vv. 20-23) and exaltation (vv. 24-26). The prayer is a beautiful glimpse of the Savior's love for His people. It also serves as an example for Christians in our future prayer for others who believe in Jesus Christ.

Other Instruction on Prayer

Other information regarding the criteria for successful prayer that Jesus provided His followers can be found in the Gospels. We must confidently pray, trusting God to answer our requests (Mark 5:25-34; 7:24-30). He told His followers to pray to God to send workers into the harvest fields (Matthew 9:38). He exhorted people to pray zealously (Matthew 26:36-39).

People who begged Jesus for different causes throughout His earthly mission did not pray to God traditionally. On the other hand, their requests and words often demonstrated different facets of prayer. Jesus established a condition for fulfilling their requests: they had to believe He could supply their needs (Matthew 8:1-4; Mark 4:35-41).

If people did not believe it, He would occasionally chastise them for their lack of faith. Therefore, praying in faith must include believing God can perform what we ask. It does not imply that He will perform anything we ask unless He has promised to do so. Praying with faith does not imply persuading ourselves that our prayers will be answered. It implies that we believe that God can accomplish everything we ask if God's will.

God delayed specific responses to pleas to test the character and encourage the endurance of those requesting (Mark 7:23). This seems to be a means of extending one's faith utilised by God throughout history (cf. Job). Finally, the grant of each prayer request is determined by God's sovereign will (Matthew 20:22). This is not to say that God's activities are entirely unexpected. In numerous cases, he has indicated what He will and will not accomplish in Scripture. To get answers to our prayers, we must pray by God's revealed will.

Importance of daily prayer

Simply said, prayer is the most appropriate way for Jesus Christ-followers to engage with God. Prayer is how we speak with the One who created us daily. The importance of everyday communication via prayer cannot be overstated. Its importance is reflected in the Bible, which mentions it more than 250 times. So, what is the purpose of daily prayer? Daily prayer helps us speak with God about all aspects of our lives. Second, daily prayer helps us express our gratitude to God for the things He gives. Third, frequent prayer lets us confess our faults and seek help overcoming them. Fourth, consistent prayer is a kind of worship and an act of obedience. Finally, daily prayer enables us to realise who is really in command of our lives. Let's take a closer look at each of these essential elements.

Daily prayer helps us speak with God about every aspect of our lives. Life's circumstances alter daily. In fact, events may swiftly develop from good to bad to worse. God urges us to bring our issues to Him for potential resolution and profit. He also asks us to share our triumphs and happiness with Him.

"Call me, and I will answer you, and show you great and difficult things, which you don't know" (Jeremiah 33:3 WEB).

God wishes that we call on Him to respond to our prayers. He also wants to reveal tremendous blessings we would have missed without praying to Him. Finally, we are urged in James 4:8 to get close to God, and he will get close to you. God desires that we stay near to Him at all times.

Praying daily allows us to show our thanks for the things He provides. It goes without saying that we must express gratitude to God for all He provides and achieves on our behalf. His benevolence and lovingkindness to us should be acknowledged every day. We are told in 1 Chronicles 16:34 to give thanks to God because he is good; his love endures forever.

In Psalm 9:1, the singer I will praise you, O LORD, with all my heart; I will tell of all your wonders. Through prayer, we appreciate His faithfulness and outstanding provision in our lives.

Daily prayer allows us to confess our sins and seek assistance in repenting them. Let's face it, whether we realise it or not, we all sin daily. So, what must we do as disciples of Jesus Christ? "Then I admitted my guilt to you and did not cover up my transgression," the Psalmist says. He continues, "I replied, 'I will confess my trespasses to the LORD,' and you absolved my sin's guilt" (Psalm 32:5). Even if God already knows, we should continue to tell Him daily. Daily prayer is an excellent location to unburden oneself from the crippling consequences of sin. So many Christians go through life with unconfessed sin that impedes our personal connection with Jesus Christ when we should humbly submit to God and seek forgiveness in prayer. Asking God for the fortitude to repent our sins is crucial for regular prayer. Only God can help us repent of our sins; for Him to do so, He must hear our repentance prayer.

Daily prayer is both a form of worship and an act of obedience. Perhaps no other passage sums up why we should pray regularly better than 1 Thessalonians 5:16-18: "Always be happy; pray constantly; offer thanks in all situations because this is God's wish for you in Christ Jesus." It is God's desire for His children to delight in Him, to pray to Him, and to offer Him gratitude. Praying without ceasing is making prayer a regular habit we never break. Prayer is also an act of worship because we show Him how much we love Him by praying to Him. In praying every day, we show obedience. It gives the Lord delight to watch His children obey His instructions.

Daily prayer is a means to recognise who is really in charge of our lives. As Christians, we understand who is really in charge. God is supreme. Nothing occurs without God's knowledge (Isaiah 46:9-10; Daniel 4:17). He is worthy of our adoration and thanks since He is the ruler over everything.

Greatness, power, glory, majesty, and grandeur are yours, O LORD, because everything in heaven and earth is yours. The dominion is yours, O LORD; you are elevated as leader over all (1 Chronicles 29:11 WEB).

God is our great King, and as such, He has complete sovereignty over our lives. Every day, we should humbly accept His rightful role in our lives and with the humility that such a great and glorious King deserves.

Finally, prayer is something that we should all strive to practise every day. However, many Christians find it difficult to humble themselves in regular prayer. Daily prayer may grow monotonous and lack adequate conviction or respect for individuals walking with the Lord for many years. Whether a beginner or a seasoned believer, prayer should always be seen as the best approach to communicating with God. Consider not speaking to a loved one or a close friend. How long do you think the relationship will last? Everyday prayer to God is daily communion with our heavenly Father. Incredibly, God would not want to interact with us at all. Indeed, the psalmist inquires, "What is a man that you are aware of him, the son of man that you care for?" (Psalm 8:4). Daily prayer is an excellent method to grasp this tremendous reality and the wonderful gift God has bestowed upon us.

Practical aspects of prayer

Is praying more appropriate while standing, sitting, kneeling, or bowing? Should we open, shut, or raise our hands to God? Do we have to close our eyes when praying? Should we pray in a church or in the open air? Should we pray first thing in the morning or at the end of the day? Is there anything more we need to mention in our prayers? Where should we begin our prayers? What is the proper way to conclude a prayer? These and other issues about prayer are often raised. What is the proper way to pray? Do any of the considerations mentioned above have any bearing?

The Proper way to pray

Prayer is often misinterpreted as a "magic formula." Some believe that God will not hear and answer our petitions if we do not correctly use the right words or pray. This is entirely contrary to the Bible. Our prayers are not answered by God based on when we pray, where we are, the position of our bodies, or how we word our petitions. In 1 John 5:14-15, we are instructed to approach God in prayer with trust, knowing He hears us and will grant us whatever we want if it is in His will.

Similarly, in John 14:13-14, Jesus declares, "And I will do everything you ask in my name, so that the Son may glorify the Father." You may make any request in my name, and I will honour it." God answers prayer requests based on whether they are made in line with His will and in the name of Jesus, according to these and other Scriptures (to bring glory to Jesus).

So, what is the proper way of praying? Philippians 4:6-7 urges us to pray without stress, for everything, and with joyful hearts. God will respond to all such pleas by bestowing the gift of His tranquilly in our hearts. The proper method to pray is to pour our souls to God, being honest and transparent with Him since He knows us better than we know ourselves. We must present our requests to God, noting that God knows what is best for us and will not positively answer a request that is not in His plan. We are to express our love, admiration, and devotion to God in prayer without stressing about using the correct words. God cares more about our hearts' content than the beauty of our words.

ACTS Prayer Formulae

Children and new Christians have been taught the ACTS prayer formula for years. ACTS is an acronym for a basic prayer format: Adoration, Confession, Thanksgiving, and Supplication. While prayer formulas may assist us in learning to pray, they do not ensure our requests will be granted. Except for the expression of gratitude, this prayer form is essentially based on the Lord's Prayer (Matthew 6:9–13).

The ACTS prayer model incorporates the following elements:

Adoration - In the ACTS paradigm, the letter A stands for adoration, equivalent to worship—glorifying and exalting God. Through adoration, we show our love and admiration for our Father. When we pray, we are instructed to worship God in devotion. This might be a song of praise to Him, a hymn of worship, a statement of His attributes, or several other types of worship.

In the ACTS paradigm, confession is symbolised by the letter C. "To agree with" is implied by confession. By confessing our sins, we agree with God that we were wrong and had sinned against Him by what we said, thought, or did. God pardons us and restores our connection with Him (1 John 1:9).

Thanksgiving is represented by the letter T. "With gratitude, make your requests known to God," Philippians 4:6 reads. (ESV). What differentiates gratitude from adoration? Worship is concerned with who God is, while thanksgiving is concerned with what God has done. We may thank God for many things, including His love, salvation, protection, and provision.

Supplication - The letter S represents supplication, prayer for our and other people's needs. A supplication is a formal request or appeal. We may ask for compassion (Psalm 4:1), direction (Psalm 5:8), knowledge (James 1:5), and a variety of other things. Paul urged us to "supplication for all the saints" (Ephesians 6:18, ESV), which translates as zealous intercessory prayer for our fellow Christian believers.

Is the ACTS prayer formula based on the Bible? The acronym does not occur in the Bible but may guide, especially when learning how to pray. Remember that prayer is not a formula, and not every prayer must cover every kind. God wishes that we express ourselves to Him and speak from our hearts. As our love for Jesus Christ develops, we naturally desire to talk to Him more.

Physical aspects of prayers

"Come, let us worship and bend down, let us kneel before the LORD our Maker," says Psalm 95:6. Bowing and kneeling have long been connected with regard and adoration (see 2 Chronicles 6:13; Psalm 138:2; Daniel 6:10). Actually, the Hebrew word for "worship" means "bow down." However, is it true that bending or kneeling is the sole acceptable position for worship or prayer?

The earliest kneeling in respect mentioned in the Bible occurred in Genesis 18:2 when three heavenly visitors arrived at Abraham. He recognised them as representing God and bowed to the ground in greeting. Pharaoh, King of Egypt, commanded all Egyptians to bow before Joseph a few generations later to symbolise respect for the formerly enslaved person raised to second-in-command (Genesis 41:42–43). As a result, very early in human history, bowing or kneeling began to indicate a modest attitude in front of someone of more significance.

By the time God handed Moses the Law, bowing and kneeling before kings and false gods had become routine. God want to establish new guidelines for worship due to Him. "You must not create for yourself an image in the shape of anything," states the second commandment. "You must not kneel down or worship them because I, the Lord your God, am a jealous God" (Exodus 20:4–5). Bowing down before someone or anything else as a form of worship is condemned by God. In Revelation 19:10, John prostrates at the feet of the angel, describing a vision to him. Still, the angel corrects him immediately: Don't do that! I am a fellow servant with you and your brothers and sisters who believe in Jesus. "Praise God!"

Worshipers in the Bible used a variety of positions, not only bowing and kneeling. Moses and Aaron knelt before the Lord, and His splendour enveloped them (Numbers 20:6). Ezekiel overcame sadness and cried out to the Lord. The Lord responded (Ezekiel 11:13–14). "Every dawn, the Levites were to stand to honour and worship the LORD." They were supposed to perform the same thing at the end of the day (1 Chronicles 23:30). David is said to have sat before the Lord to pray (2 Samuel 7:18). When Jesus gave His most extended recorded prayer, He "lifted His gaze toward heaven" (John 17), and Paul advised, "men everywhere to pray, raising up holy hands without wrath or arguing" (1 Timothy 2:8). The Bible teaches that there is more than one correct position for worship or prayer.

While physical expressions of worship are vital, and we should worship God with our whole being, the condition of our hearts is more important than the stance of our bodies. When our emotions are in a state of humility and wonder, our bodies frequently yearn to reflect that in tangible ways. Kneeling, kneeling, laying facedown, bending our heads, and raising our hands are outward manifestations of our inner dispositions. Of course, bodily activities are meaningless without a matching heart position. Psalm 51:17 wonderfully describes God's intention for our worship: "The offerings of God are a broken soul; O God, You will not disdain a broken and a contrite heart."

True worship is a way of life, not just an activity. While devoted moments of intensive connection with God are necessary for our spiritual health, we are also instructed to "pray without stopping" (1 Thessalonians 5:17). Paul admonishes believers to see their bodies as living sacrifices (Romans 12:1–2), and our souls should be overflowing with psalms, hymns, and spiritual songs, singing and making melody to the Lord with your heart; always giving thanks to God, to the Father for all things (Ephesians 5:19–20). Even as we go about our daily lives, our hearts may be in a constant state of praise and prayer. "The objective of every Christian should be to live in uninterrupted devotion," A. W. Tozer remarked. Kneeling, bowing, laying down, and strolling along the street are all postures of prayer and worship acceptable to God when that is our objective.

Accordingly, the Lord's Prayer in Matthew 6:9-13 comes the closest to offering a "pattern" for prayer in the Bible. Please remember that we should not memorise and recite the Lord's Prayer to God. Worship, trust in God, requests, confession, and submission are all things that should be included in prayer. We are to pray for the things described in the Lord's Prayer in our own words, "personalising" it to our relationship with God. The proper way to pray is to express our emotions to God. Sitting, standing, or kneeling; hands open or closed; eyes open or closed; at a church, home, or outdoors; early or late—all of these are secondary issues that must be measured against personal choice, conviction, and appropriateness. God desires prayer to be a sincere and personal connection between Him and us.

Elements of Prayer

Adoration

A theology of worship is a theory about God's worship; a biblical theology of worship only focuses on what the Bible states. Just as biblical soteriology is founded on the Bible's entire teaching on salvation, biblical theology of worship is founded on the Bible's comprehensive teaching on God's worship and adoration.

It is critical to have a biblical theology of worship. Not everything labelled "worship" is genuine worship, as Cain and Abel discovered in the beginning: "the Lord looked with favour on Abel and his offering, but he did not look with favour on Cain and his offering" (Genesis 4:4–5). What was Cain's issue (apart from jealousy, stubbornness, and deadly anger)? He lacks a suitable worship theology. Cain presented an unsuitable offering to the Lord and requested that he be pleased.

The church that does not follow biblical worship theology risks failing to give God honour and offer acceptable worship to Him. Worship is as misunderstood as any other concept in the church. Contrary to common assumption, worship does not begin and conclude with the singing section of our church services. Worship is also more than just kneeling in adoration before God. To begin with, God determines worship, not our sincerity, religious thoughts, or musical ability.

Hebrews 12:28 says we must "serve God acceptably with respect and holy dread" (NKJV). The Greek word for "serve" here is a variant of the Greek word for worship, and it appears 21 times in the New Testament in settings of service and worship. Another term for worship is therapeutic, derived from the Greek word therapeutic and is most typically rendered "heal" concerning the healing of others. This term appears in several texts in the New Testament describing Jesus' healing.

Other Greek meanings for "worship" include proskuneó, which means "paying tribute" (1 Corinthians 14:25), sebázomai, which means "to show religious respect" (Romans 1:25), and sébomai, which means "to revere or admire" (Acts 16:14). We find a variant of the term sébomai employed by Jesus, to foolish, hypocritical worship of God (Matthew 15:9), meaning that "worship of God" is not always what it seems to be.

The sincere worship of God is the focus of a biblical theology of worship. True biblical worship must be awe-inspiring (Hebrews 12:28). We need to know who is being adored. To name a few attributes, God is holy, just, perfect, powerful, and loving. We are sinners redeemed by grace who come before a holy God via our Redeemer. There is no space for arrogance (see Luke 18:9–14). Worship must also be "true," so our worship must be appropriately informed (John 4:24). There can be no true worship until we precisely understand the God we serve. According to the Bible, those seeking to worship must worship God as He is presented. Unbiblical perspectives about God must be rejected.

A biblical theology of worship acknowledges that worship entails more than just externals. "These people come... honour me with their lips, but their hearts are distant from me," God says. Their devotion to me is based only on human norms that they have been taught" (Isaiah 29:13). Worship is neither about ritual nor creativity. However, both may be legitimate forms of worship. Although David's "dancing before the LORD with all his might" was an act of genuine devotion, worship is not about expressing oneself (2 Samuel 6:14). Worship is not about music, but worshippers often employ music. True worship is focused on God. We regard, honour, and worship Him for what He does for us and who He is.

Worship that generates a heart transformation results from a biblical theology of worship. The worshiper's desire to love and follow the Lord will become stronger. Worship and service go hand in hand;

worshipping God should motivate us to do more. Those who love Jesus will obey His commands, according to Jesus (John 14:15). Our worship is pointless if we declare we love and adore Him yet do not follow Him.

A biblical understanding of worship promotes the belief that worship is a way of life, not a passing fad (see 1 Corinthians 10:31). Our lives are to be devoted to God's worship and service. Worship is more than a one-time, experience-oriented activity on Sunday, followed by a return to "regular" living for the rest of the week. True worship is continuous, inner praise to the God of the Scriptures, expressed through prayer, music, service, giving, and living.

Confession

"What happens if I offend and then die before I get a chance to confess my sin to God?" is a frequently asked question. Another often-asked issue is, "What happens if I commit a sin but then forget about it and never confess it to God?" Both of these queries are based on an incorrect assumption. Salvation does not include Christians confessing and repenting every sin they commit before death. Salvation is not determined by whether or not a Christian admits and repents every sin. Yes, we must confess our sins to God as soon as we realise we have done so. However, we do not always have to beg God's pardon. All of our sins are forgiven when we trust Jesus Christ for salvation. This encompasses everything from the past, present, and future, whether large or tiny. Believers do not have to continually beg for forgiveness or repent of being forgiven of their sins. When Jesus died to pay the punishment for our sins, they were all forgiven (Colossians 1:14; Acts 10:43).

We must confess our faults:

If we confess our sins, he is faithful and righteous to forgive and cleanse us from all unrighteousness. (1 John 1:9 WEB).

This text instructs us to "confess" our faults to God. To confess implies to agree with. By confessing our sins to God, we acknowledge the truth that we were wrong, that we had sinned. God forgives us continuously via confession because He is faithful and righteous. What does it mean for God to be faithful and just? He is loyal by forgiving sins, as He has promised to do for those who accept Christ as their Savior. He is just because he applies Christ's atonement for our sins, indicating that our sins have been redressed.

Furthermore, 1 John 1:9 implies that God's forgiveness is contingent on admitting our faults to Him. How does this work if we are all forgiven of our sins the instant we accept Christ as our Savior? The apostle John seems to be saying "relational" forgiveness. Our sins are "positionally" forgiven instantly when we accept Christ as Savior. This positional forgiveness ensures our salvation and promises an everlasting abode in paradise. God will not reject our entry into paradise because of our sins when we stand before Him after death. That is what situational forgiveness entails. The idea behind relational forgiveness is that when we sin, we insult God and hurt His Spirit (Ephesians 4:30). While God has eventually forgiven us for our sins, they nonetheless provide a stumbling block or barrier in our relationship with God. A young kid who commits a transgression against his father is not expelled from the household. A good parent will unreservedly forgive his children. At the same time, a healthy father-son connection cannot be created unless the relationship is healed. This can only happen if a youngster admits and apologises to his father for his misdeeds. For this reason, we confess our sins to God—not to keep our salvation, but to reestablish a personal connection with the God who loves us and has already forgiven us.

Thanksgiving

Thankfulness is a significant motif in the Bible. "Be happy continuously; pray continually; give thanks in all situations, because this is God's wish for you in Christ Jesus," reads First Thessalonians 5:16-18. Did you notice what I said? Thank you in all cases.

Thankfulness should be a natural part of our lives, flowing effortlessly from our hearts and tongues.

We can learn why we should be grateful and thankful in various situations by delving further into the Scriptures.

"Give thanks to the Lord, because he is good," says Psalm 136:1. His love lasts forever." We have two reasons to be grateful in this situation: God's consistent kindness and unwavering love. When we acknowledge the nature of our sinfulness and realise that there is only death apart from God (John 10:10; Romans 7:5), our natural reaction is to be thankful for the life He provides.

Psalm 30 expresses gratitude to God for His rescue.

I will extol you, Yahweh, for you have raised me and not made my foes rejoice over me. Yahweh, my God, I cried to you, and you have healed me. Yahweh, you have brought up my soul from Sheol. You have kept me alive, that I should not go down to the pit. Sing praise to Yahweh, you saints of his. Give thanks to his holy name. For his anger is but for a moment. His favour is for a lifetime. Weeping may stay for the night, but joy comes in the morning. As for me, I said in my prosperity, "I shall never be moved." You, Yahweh, when you favoured me, made my mountain stand strong, but when you hid your face, I was troubled. I cried to you, Yahweh. I supplicated to the Lord: "What profit is there in my destruction if I go down to the pit? Shall the dust praise you? Shall it declare your truth? Hear, Yahweh, and have mercy on me. Yahweh, be my helper." You have turned my mourning into dancing for me. You have removed my sackcloth and clothed me with gladness. Ultimately, my heart may sing praise to you and not be silent. Yahweh, my God, I will give thanks to you forever! (Psalm 30:1-12 WEB).

David expresses his gratitude to God in this passage after an apparently painful event. This psalm of gratitude praises God in the present and recalls God's faithfulness in the past. It is a declaration of God's character, which is so lovely that only praise is suitable.

We also have instances of being appreciative in the face of adversity. Psalm 28 illustrates David's anguish, for example. It's pleading with God for compassion, protection, and justice.

Blessed be Yahweh because he has heard the voice of my petitions. Yahweh is my strength and my shield. My heart has trusted in him, and I am helped. Therefore, my heart greatly rejoices. With my song, I will thank him. (Psalm 28:6-7 WEB).

Amid adversity, David recalls God and expresses gratitude for knowing and believing in God. Even in the face of death, Job maintained a similar attitude of praise:

Yahweh gave, and Yahweh has taken away. Blessed be Yahweh's name (Job 1:21 WEB).

There are several instances of Christians' gratitude in the New Testament. Paul said that God always leads us in triumphal procession in Christ despite being persecuted and disseminates the fragrance of his knowledge through us. (2 Corinthians 2:14). As a result, because we are receiving an unshakeable kingdom, the writer of Hebrews says, let us be thankful and worship God acceptably with reverence and awe (Hebrews 12:28). Peter gives us a reason to rejoice amid loss and adversity, noting that it is through these that our faith will be proved genuine and result in praise, glory, and honour when Jesus Christ is revealed (1 Peter 1:6-7).

God's people are grateful because they know how much they have been given. According to 2 Timothy 3:2, one of the hallmarks of the latter days is a lack of thankfulness. Wicked individuals will be "ungrateful."

We should be grateful because God is deserving of our praise. It is only natural to give Him credit for "every good and perfect gift" He bestows (James 1:17). When we are appreciative, our attention shifts away from selfish aspirations and the misery of our present situation. Expressing gratitude reminds us that God is in charge. So, being thankful is not only acceptable; it is also healthy and good for us.

It reminds us of the more comprehensive picture: we belong to God and have received all spiritual blessings (Ephesians 1:3). We enjoy an abundant life (John 10:10), so gratitude is appropriate.'

Supplication

We pray to God for several reasons, including worshipping Him, confessing our faults and asking for forgiveness, thanking Him for His benefits, requesting things for ourselves, and/or praying for the needs of others. The Hebrew and Greek terms most typically translated as "supplication" in the Bible literally mean "a request or plea," therefore, a prayer of supplication is a request to God. Unlike a petition prayer, a request for someone else, a supplication prayer is often a desire for the person praying.

Many supplication prayers are found in the Bible. The Psalms have several instances. David's psalms are loaded with requests for mercy (Psalm 4:1), leadership (Psalm 5:8), deliverance (Psalm 6:4), and redemption from affliction (Psalm 7:1), among other things. When Daniel discovered that Monarch Darius had issued an order forbidding prayer to any deity other than the king, he continued to pray to God in thankfulness and request His aid in this challenging circumstance.

In the New Testament, Jesus advises us in Matthew 6:11 to beg for our daily food, which comes under the category of a prayer of supplication. Furthermore, in Luke 18:1-8, Jesus encourages us not to stop asking for what we need. According to James, on the one hand, we do not get because we do not ask (James 4:2). We ask but do not get on the other side because we are simply concerned with our fleshly wants (James 4:3). Perhaps the best method to approach supplications is to ask God, in all honesty, as if you were a kid speaking to a loving Father. Still, closing with "You will be done" (Matthew 26:39), in complete submission to His will.

After emphasising the need to don the "whole armour of God" (Ephesians 6:13-17), the apostle Paul admonished the Ephesians (and us) to be vigilant and to pray in the Spirit, interceding for the saints (Ephesians 6:18). Clearly, supplication prayers are part of all Christians' spiritual war. Paul encourages the Philippian church to ease their anxiety by praying faithfully, particularly thanksgiving and supplication. He adds that this is the prescription for assuring that In Christ Jesus, the peace of God that transcends all explanation will protect your hearts and minds. (Philippians 4:6-7).

Another essential aspect of supplication prayer is the requirement for faith in the Lord Jesus Christ. Those who belong to Christ are indwelt by the Holy Spirit, who intercedes on our behalf. We don't always know what or how to pray when we come to God. The Spirit intercedes and prays for us, perceiving our supplications so that when we are weighed down by trials and the concerns of life, He comes alongside us to lend assistance with our supplication prayers as He sustains us before the throne of grace (Romans 8:26).

Types of Prayers

The Bible shows many different prayers and uses several terms to express them. 1 Timothy 2:1 (WEB), for example, reads,

I exhort, therefore, first of all, that petitions, prayers, intercessions, and givings of thanks be made for all men:

All four basic Greek terms for prayer are given in this line. The following are the primary kinds of prayers found in the Bible:

Prayer for healing: "And the prayer of faith will rescue the one who is sick, and the Lord will raise him up," James 5:15 states. In this context, prayer is given in trust for a sick person, asking God to cure them. We must trust in God's power and kindness (Mark 9:23).

The agreement prayer (also known as corporate prayer): The disciples "all came together frequently in prayer" after Jesus' ascension (Acts 1:14). Following Pentecost, the early church "dedicated themselves" to prayer (Acts 2:42). Their example inspires us to pray with others.

The request prayer (or supplication): We bring our petitions to God. Do not be worried about anything; Philippians 4:6 says, But in everything, make your requests known to God through prayer and petition with thankfulness. Praying in the Spirit is part of winning the spiritual fight (Ephesians 6:18).

The prayer of thanksgiving: In Philippians 4:6, we discover another prayer: thanksgiving or gratitude to God. "Make your petitions known to God with thankfulness." The Psalms provide several instances of gratitude prayers.

The worship prayer: The worship prayer is comparable to the gratitude prayer. Worship focuses on who God is, while gratitude focuses on what God has done. "While they were worshipping the Lord and fasting, the Holy Spirit said, 'Set apart for me Barnabas and Saul for the job to which I have called them,'" church leaders in Antioch prayed. After fasting and praying, they placed their hands on them and sent them out" (Acts 13:2-3).

The Consecration Prayer: Sometimes, prayer is a moment to separate ourselves from the world to follow God's will. "And going a little further, he dropped on his face and prayed, saying, 'My Father, if it is possible, let this cup pass from me; nonetheless, not as I will, but as you will,'" Jesus said the night before His crucifixion. (Matthew 26:39, NIV)

Intercession prayer: Our prayers often contain requests for others as we intercede for them. In 1 Timothy 2:1, we pray "for everyone." In this regard, Jesus is our model. The chapter of John 17 is Jesus' plea on behalf of His followers and all Christians.

Imprecatory prayer: Imprecatory prayers are found throughout the Psalms (e.g., 7, 55, 69). They are employed to call down God's wrath on the wicked and avenge the virtuous. The psalmists use this form of a plea to stress God's holiness and the certainty of His judgment. Jesus encourages us to pray for blessings on our adversaries rather than condemning them (Matthew 5:44-48).

The Bible also mentions praying in the Spirit (1 Corinthians 14:14-15) and praying when we lack good words (Romans 8:26-27). During such times, the Spirit Himself intercedes for us.

Prayer is a communication with God that should be done continuously (1 Thessalonians 5:16-18). We will naturally want to speak to Jesus Christ as our love for Him grows.

Prayer as an act of worship

In Romans 12:1-2 (WEB), the apostle Paul accurately expressed authentic worship:

Therefore, I urge you, brothers, by the mercies of God, to present your bodies as a living sacrifice, holy, acceptable to God, which is your spiritual service. Don't be conformed to this world, but be transformed by renewing your mind so that you may prove God's good, well-pleasing, and perfect will.

This verse encompasses every aspect of genuine adoration. First, the reason for worship is "God's mercies." God's mercies include everything He has given us that we do not deserve, including everlasting love, everlasting grace, the Holy Spirit, everlasting peace, everlasting joy, saving faith, comfort, strength, wisdom, hope, patience, kindness, honour, glory, righteousness, security, eternal life, forgiveness, reconciliation, justification, sanctification, freedom, intercession, and much more. The knowledge and comprehension of these tremendous blessings inspire us to offer praise and thanksgiving—in other words, to worship!

The verse also describes how we should worship: "present your bodies as a living and holy sacrifice." Presenting our bodies is giving God our whole selves. The allusion to our bodies here refers to all our human capacities—our hearts, brains, hands, ideas, and attitudes—which are to be surrendered to God. In other words, we are to relinquish control of these things and hand them up to Him, just as a real sacrifice was wholly surrendered to God on the altar. But how exactly? The text is plain once more: "by the renewing of your mind." We refresh our brains regularly by purging them of the world's "knowledge" and replacing it with real wisdom from God. We worship Him with our brains that have been regenerated and purified, not our emotions. Emotions are lovely things, but they can be destructive, out-of-control energies unless fashioned by a mind immersed in Truth.

Where the intellect goes, the will follows, and the emotions follow as well. According to First Corinthians 2:16, we have "the intellect of Christ," not "the emotions of Christ."

The only method to rejuvenate our thoughts is via the Word of God. It is the truth, the knowledge of God's Word, which is the knowledge of God's mercies, and we are back where we started. Knowing the truth, believing the truth, having Biblical convictions, and loving the truth will naturally lead to authentic spiritual worship. Conviction leads to attachment; affection reacts to the truth, not external stimuli, including music. Music in and of itself has nothing to do with adoration. Music cannot generate worship, but it may indeed induce feeling. Music does not create worship, but it may express it. Don't rely on music to encourage your worship; instead, look to music as an expression of what is caused by a heart rapt by God's mercies and obedient to His instructions.

True worship is concentrated on God. People are often preoccupied with where they should worship, what music they should sing, and how their worship seems to others. Concentrating on these details misses the purpose entirely. According to Jesus, true worshippers will worship God in spirit and truth (John 4:24). This implies that we worship from the heart and in the manner that God intended. Praying, reading God's Word with an open heart, singing, partaking in communion, and helping others are all examples of worship. It is not confined to a single act but is done correctly for its heart and mentality.

It's also crucial to understand that worship is just for God. Only He, not any of His servants, is worthy (Revelation 19:10). Saints, prophets, statues, angels, false gods, or Mary, Jesus' mother, are not worshipped. We should also not worship with the anticipation of receiving anything in return, such as a miracle cure. Worship is performed only for God's delight (because He deserves it). Worship may be public praise to God (Psalm 22:22; 35:18) in a congregational setting, where we can express our admiration and thanks to Him and all He has done for us via prayer and praise. True adoration is sensed internally and then exhibited outwardly. "Worshiping" for "worshipping" is displeasing to God and entirely in vain. He sees right through all of the hypocrisy and despises it. He displays this in Amos 5:21-24 when He speaks of the approaching judgement.

Another example is the tale of Cain and Abel, Adam and Eve's first sons. They both offered gifts to the Lord, but only Abel's was accepted. Cain provided the gift out of duty, whereas Abel brought his best lambs. He expressed his faith and adoration for God.

True worship is more than just what we do in church or open praise (although these things are good and told in the Bible to do them). True worship recognises God and all His power and splendour in everything we do. Obedience to Him and His Word is the ultimate form of praise and adoration. We must know God to achieve this; we cannot be ignorant of Him (Acts 17:23). Worship is glorifying and exalting God—expressing our love and adoration for our heavenly Father.

Power of Prayer

The notion that power is inherent in prayer is widely held. According to the Bible, prayer is simply the power of God, who hears and answers prayer. Take into account the following:

1) The Lord God Almighty can accomplish anything; nothing is impossible for Him (Luke 1:37).

2) The Almighty God asks His people to pray to Him. Prayer to God should be made constantly (Luke 18:1), with gratitude (Philippians 4:6), in confidence (James 1:5), within God's will (Matthew 6:10), for God's glory (John 14:13-14), and from a righteous heart (James 5:16).

3) The Lord God Almighty hears His children's petitions. He tells us to pray and promises to hear us when we do. "In my anguish, I cried out to the LORD; I begged my God for aid." He heard my voice from his temple, and my scream came before him, into his ears" (Psalm 18:6).

4) The Lord God Almighty responds to prayer. "I call on you, O God, and you will respond to me" (Psalm 17:6). "When the righteous cry out, the LORD hears them, and he saves them from all their woes" (Psalm 34:17).

Another widely held belief is that our faith level influences whether God will answer our requests. However, the Lord occasionally answers our requests despite our lack of confidence. The congregation prays for Peter's release from jail in Acts 12 (v. 5), and God fulfils their request (vv. 7-11). Peter knocks on the door of the prayer gathering, but those who are praying first refuse to accept it is Peter. They prayed for his release but didn't anticipate a response to their prayers.

The power of prayer does not come from us; it is not due to the specific words we speak, the particular method we say them, or even the frequency with which we repeat them. The power of prayer is not dependent on the direction we face or the posture of our body. Using objects, icons, candles, or beads does not increase the power of prayer. The power of prayer comes from the almighty One who hears and answers our requests. Prayer brings us into touch with Almighty God. We should anticipate Almighty outcomes, whether He grants or refuses our prayers. Whatever the outcome of our petitions, the God to whom we pray is the source of prayer's power, and He can and will respond to us according to His perfect will and time.

Conditions for Effective Prayer

Some folks want prayer without any conditions. They see God as a magical genie who must fulfil every request they make when called via prayer. They take solace in the storey of Aladdin, and his lamp aspires to that degree of control over God's power in their prayer life. However, the Bible teaches that prayer is subject to certain restrictions. If you believe, Jesus continued, you will get anything you ask for in prayer (Matthew 21:22). Even in that statement, there is one requirement for prayer: trust. When we analyse the Bible, we see additional requirements for prayer.

Here are eight biblical commandments on prayer that suggest requirements for praying:

1) Pray to God the Father (Matthew 6:9). This prayer prerequisite may seem apparent, yet it is critical. We do not pray to false gods, ourselves, angels, Buddha, or the Virgin Mary. We pray to the Bible's God, who revealed Himself in Jesus Christ and whose Spirit lives within us. Coming to Him as our "Father" emphasises that we are first and foremost His children, having been made such by trust in Christ (see John 1:12).

2) Ask for excellent things (Matthew 7:11). We don't always understand or recognise what is good, but God does, and He is glad to provide what is best for His children. Paul prayed three times for healing from an ailment, and each time, God responded, "No." Why would a loving God deny Paul's healing? Because God had something greater in mind for him, namely a grace-filled existence. Paul started to revel in his weakness rather than pray for a cure (2 Corinthians 12:7–10).

3) Pray for things in need (see Philippians 4:19). One of the prerequisites for prayer is to prioritise God's kingdom (Matthew 6:33). The promise is that God will meet all of our necessities, not all of our desires. There is a distinction.

4) Pray with a pure heart (see James 5:16). The Bible mentions having a clean conscience as a prerequisite for answering your prayers (Hebrews 10:22). We must confess our faults to the Lord. "The Lord will not hear if I consider evil in my heart" (Psalm 66:18, NAS).

5) Pray with a thankful heart (see Philippians 4:6). An attitude of thankfulness is part of prayer.

6) Pray per God's will (see 1 John 5:14). A crucial need for prayer is that it be prayed within the will of God. "Not my will, but your will be done," Jesus prayed all the time, even in Gethsemane (Luke 22:42). We may pray all we want for XYZ with great sincerity and trust. Still, if God's will is ABC, we are praying incorrectly.

7) Pray in the name of Jesus Christ (see John 16:24). We may approach the throne of grace because of Jesus (Hebrews 10:19–22). He is our mediator (1 Timothy 2:5). One of the requirements for prayer is that we pray in His name.

8) Keep praying (Luke 18:1). In fact, never stop praying (1 Thessalonians 5:17). One of the requirements for successful prayer is that we not give up.

9) Pray without self-interest (see James 4:3). Our motivations are crucial.

10) Pray with trust (James 1:6). Without faith, it is impossible to satisfy God (Hebrews 11:6), who alone can do the impossible (Luke 1:37). Why pray if you don't believe?

Joshua's courageous plea for the sun to remain still satisfied all these prayer criteria (Joshua 10:12–14). All of these prerequisites were satisfied by Elijah's petition for the rain to be withheld and his subsequent plea for the rain to fall (James 5:17–18). These prerequisites were satisfied by Jesus' prayer as He stood by Lazarus' grave (John 11:41). According to His will, they all prayed to God in confidence for good and essential things.

The stories of Joshua, Elijah, and Jesus demonstrate that beautiful things happen when our prayers align with God's sovereign will.

Mountains should not be feared since they can be moved (Mark 11:23). The difficulty we encounter is aligning our prayers with God's will and having our wishes meet His. The objective is for God's will to be congruent with our own. We desire nothing more or less than what He wants. And we are not interested in anything that He is not interested in.

Godly, effective prayer is subject to unavoidable circumstances, and God urges us to pray. When can we pray? When we feel God desires something significant. When can we pray boldly? When we feel God desires something daring. When are we supposed to pray? All the time.

All believers want their prayers to be effective, so focusing on the results of our prayers causes us to lose sight of our unique gift in prayer. The fact that someone like us can communicate with the world's Creator is incredible in and of itself. Even more impressive is that He hears us and acts on our behalf! We must first understand that successful prayer is that our Lord and Savior, Jesus Christ, had to suffer and die on the cross before we could ever approach the throne of grace to worship and pray (Hebrews 10:19-25).

Although the Bible provides many directions on strengthening our relationship with the Creator, successful prayer has more to do with who is praying than with "how" we are to pray. Indeed, Scripture states that "the prayer of a virtuous man is strong and effective" (James 5:16), that "the Lord's eyes are on the righteous, and his ears are listening to their petition" (1 Peter 3:12; Psalm 34:15), and that "the prayer of the upright pleases Him" (Proverbs 15:8). Prayer delivered the righteous Daniel from the lion's den (Daniel 6:11). God's chosen people benefited from Moses' good standing with God in the wilderness (Exodus 16–17). The barren Hannah's persistent and modest prayers produced the prophet Samuel (1 Samuel 1:20), while the apostle Paul's prayers caused earthquakes (Acts 16:25-26). The fervent prayers of God's righteous children can achieve a great deal (Numbers 11:2).

We must ensure that our prayers are following God's will. "This is our assurance when approaching God: that if we ask anything according to His will, he hears us" (1 John 5:14-15). Praying in line with God's will is simply praying under what He would like, and God's revealed will may be found throughout Scripture. Suppose we are unsure what to pray for. In that case, Paul reminds us that as God's children, we may depend on the Holy Spirit to intercede for us, for the Spirit intercedes for the saints per God's desire (Romans 8:27). And, since the Spirit of God understands God's thoughts, the Spirit's petition is always under the Father's desire.

Furthermore, prayer is something that Christians should practise "ongoingly" (1 Thessalonians 5:17). Luke tells us to pray persistently and not give up (Luke 18:1). In addition, as we bring our petitions to God, we are to pray with trust (James 1:5; Mark 11:22-24), gratitude (Philippians 4:6), forgive others (Mark 11:25), in Christ's name (John 14:13-14), and, as previously indicated, with a righteous heart (James 5:16). It is the power of our faith, not the length of our prayers, that pleases Him; therefore, we don't need to impress God with our eloquence or knowledge. God knows what we need before we ask (Matthew 6:8).

Also, as we pray, we should ensure no unconfessed sin in our minds since this would undoubtedly be a barrier to successful prayer.

But your iniquities have separated you and your God, and your sins have hidden his face from you so that he will not hear. (Isaiah 59:2 WEB; see also Psalm 66:18 WEB).

God promises that if we confess our sins, He will forgive us and instil righteousness within us (1 John 1:9).

Praying for selfish reasons and wrong motivations is another impediment to successful contact with God. "When you ask, you do not get because you ask with the wrong motivations, intending to spend what you receive on your pleasures" (James 4:3). Rejecting God's call or rejecting His guidance (Proverbs 1:24-28), idol worship

(Jeremiah 11:11-14), or ignoring the needy (Proverbs 21:13) are all barriers to successful prayer.

Effective prayer is a means of strengthening our connection with our heavenly Father. When we study and follow His Word and endeavour to please Him, the same God who caused the sun to stop shining on Joshua's request (Joshua 10:12-13) urges us to approach confidently before the throne of grace and pray with confidence that He will extend His mercy and grace to aid us in our time of need (Hebrews 4:16).

Obstacles to effective prayer

The unconfessed sins of the one praying are the most visible impediments to a powerful prayer life. When we approach God with unconfessed sin in our lives, there is a barrier between Him and us because our God is holy. However, sins have distanced us from God, while crimes have hidden his face so that he cannot hear our prayers (Isaiah 59:2). "If I had treasured sin in my heart, the Lord would not have listened," David agreed, knowing from experience that God is distant from people who attempt to conceal their wrongdoing:

If I cherished sin in my heart, the Lord wouldn't have listened (Psalm 66:18 WEB).

Scripture mentions numerous types of sin that are impediments to effective prayer. For starters, when we live according to the flesh rather than the Spirit, we lose our desire to pray and our capacity to properly connect with God. Although we are born again with a new nature, that new nature remains in our old body, and that old "tent" is corrupt and wicked. Unless we are vigilant to put to death the works of the body (Romans 8:13) and be led by the Spirit in an authentic relationship with God, the flesh may obtain control of our actions, attitudes, and intentions. Then, will we be able to communicate with Him through an intimate connection.

Selfishness is one way that life in the body presents itself and is also an obstacle to successful prayer. Our intentions stymie our petitions when we pray selfishly and ask God for what we desire rather than what He wants.

This is the boldness which we have toward him, that, if we ask anything according to his will, he listens to us. (1 John 5:14 WEB).

Asking according to God's will is the same as asking in surrender to whatever His will is, whether we know what that will is or not. Like in everything else, Jesus is to be our model in prayer. He constantly prayed in His Father's will: "Yet not my will, but yours be done" (Luke

22:42). Selfish prayers are always meant to please our selfish wants, and we should not expect God to react to them.

You do not get when you ask with the wrong motivations, intending to spend what you receive on your pleasures (James 4:3 WEB).

Living for selfish, fleshly pleasures can also obstruct our prayers because it generates a hard heart toward others. We may expect God to be indifferent to our needs if we are insensitive to the needs of others. When we pray to God, our primary concern should be His will. The second consideration should be the needs of others. This originates from the belief that we consider others more significant than ourselves and prioritise their interests above our own (Philippians 2:3-4).

Unforgiveness toward others is a fundamental impediment to successful prayer. When we refuse to forgive others, a bitter root develops in our hearts and chokes our prayers. Suppose we retain anger and resentment against others. How can we expect God to shower His benefits on us unworthy sinners? This notion is vividly demonstrated in Matthew 18:23-35's narrative of the unforgiving servant. This narrative reminds us that God has forgiven us an incalculable debt (our sin) and wants us to forgive others as we have been forgiven. Refusing to do so will impede our prayers.

Unbelief and uncertainty are other significant impediments to effective prayer. This does not imply, as some claim, that God is compelled to fulfil our prayers because we come to Him believing He will. Praying without hesitation entails having firm confidence in and knowledge of God's character, nature, and motivations.

Without faith, it is impossible to be well pleasing to him, for he who comes to God must believe that he exists and that he is a rewarder of those who seek him. (Hebrews 11:6 WEB).

When we approach God in prayer with doubts about His character, purpose, and promises, we severely disrespect Him. Our trust must be in His power to grant any request consistent with His plan and purpose for our lives. We must pray that whatever He intends is the greatest possible situation.

But let him ask in faith, without doubting, for he who doubts is like a wave of the sea, driven by the wind and tossed. That man shouldn't think he will receive anything from the Lord (James 1:6-7 WEB).

Finally, domestic strife is a significant impediment to prayer. Peter especially mentions this as an obstacle to the prayers of a husband with a less-than-godly attitude toward his wife. Husbands, be mindful of how you treat your wives and regard them as the weaker companions and co-heirs with you of the wonderful gift of life so that nothing prevents your prayers (1 Peter 3:7). When there is substantial disagreement in family ties and the head of the home does not exhibit the attitudes mentioned by Peter, the husband's prayer connection with God is hampered. Similarly, ladies must adhere to biblical ideals of submitting to their husbands' authority if their prayers are not hampered (Ephesians 5:22-24).

Fortunately, these prayer impediments may be addressed simultaneously by approaching God in confession and repentance petitions. In 1 John 1:9, we are guaranteed that if we confess our sins, he is trustworthy and just and will forgive our sins and cleanse us from all unrighteousness. After that, we have a clear and open line of contact with God, and our prayers are not only heard and answered. Still, they are also filled with an incredible feeling of delight.

Fervent Prayer

The phrase "fervent prayer" derives from the King James Version's James 5:16: "The effective, fervent prayer of a righteous man availeth much." The definition of ardent in English is "impassioned, forceful, passionate, sincere, powerful, or wholehearted." The passage suggests that a passionate, wholehearted prayer would achieve much, meaning that a half-hearted prayer will not be as powerful.

Most modern versions translate James 5:16 so that the fervency or forcefulness refers to the outcome of the prayer rather than the earnestness of the prayer: "The prayer of a righteous person has great power as it works" (ESV); "The prayer of a righteous person is powerful and effective" (NIV); "The effective prayer of a righteous man can accomplish much" (NASB). These translations simply state that prayer is powerful without distinguishing between "fervent" and other types of prayer.

This enlarged paraphrase may help to clarify the difference: "A virtuous man's prayer will achieve much" vs "A righteous man's prayer will bring strong, powerful effects."

The variation in translation seems to be centred on the correct placement of the phrase translated "fervent," "powerful," or "effective." The KJV and NKJV read the text so that it refers to the kind of prayer—an ardent, strong, or powerful prayer may achieve a lot. The modifier is applied to the outcome of the prayer rather than the petition itself in the other versions—it will have a solid or robust consequence. So, the KJV and NKJV urge people to pray sincerely for their prayers to be answered. Still, the other translations encourage people to pray because the effects may be vital.

The context aids in elucidating the intended meaning. The immediate context mentions praying for healing and promises that "prayer of faith" (faithful prayer) would be answered. The first section of James 5:16 states that we should confess our faults and pray for one another's healing. The second portion of the stanza seems to summarise the notion. Then, in lines 17–18, an example of the recommended kind of prayer is given. Elijah, like us, was a human being. He prayed sincerely that it would not rain, and it did not rain for three and a half years on the land. He prayed again; the skies provided rain, and the ground produced crops.

In 1 Kings 17:1, Elijah promised Ahab that it would not rain "for the next several years." This famine was God's punishment for Israel's worship of Baal. After three and a half years of drought, Elijah fought the prophets of Baal in a battle on Mt. Carmel (1 Kings 18:16–40), and Elijah then assured King Ahab that it would rain (verse 41).

"Ahab walked out to eat and drink, but Elijah ascended to the summit of Carmel, knelt down, and placed his face between his knees. 'Go gaze toward the water,' he said to his servant." And he stepped up to have a look. "'There's nothing there,' he said. "'Go back,' Elijah commanded seven times." "The servant reported the seventh time, 'A cloud as tiny as a man's palm is rising from the sea.' "So Elijah told Ahab, "Hitch up your chariot and go down before the rain stops you." "Meanwhile, the sky darkened with clouds, the wind increased, a heavy rain began to pour, and Ahab rode out to Jezreel" (1 Kings 18:42–45 WEB).

On Mt. Carmel, Elijah declared that it would rain and then prayed for it to rain. He prayed seven times for rain. He dispatched his servant to check the sky after each prayer to see whether it would rain. If that didn't work, he'd pray again. After the seventh time, a little cloud appeared, which Elijah mistook for the answer to his prayer—and it was. He had prayed while knelt on the ground, his face between his knees. This might be construed as a heartfelt supplication.

Considering all the facts, fervency may not be the most crucial aspect of prayer. Elijah indeed prayed diligently. However, James' message seems to be more focused on the effectiveness of prayer and the element of holiness in the person praying. The requirement to confess sins precedes the advice to pray. James further emphasises that the prayer is coming from a good person. Elijah was a virtuous man, and the outcome of his request was remarkable.

The purpose of James 5:13–18 is that prayer is vital, and God answers prayer; therefore, we should prioritise it. We are not required to be "super Christians." We could be tempted to think of Elijah as a great saint, but James argues he was just an average guy who prayed, and God replied. However, sin in the life of the person praying might obstruct the efficacy of prayer. Certainly, sincere prayer and prayer of faith are necessary. Still, this verse does not imply that the energy with which one prays affects efficacy. Instead, a virtuous person's prayer is strong (forceful) and effective.

We should repent of our misdeeds and pray, expecting God to respond. Of course, we should not pray half-heartedly or casually, and other verses exhort us to pray with perseverance (Matthew 7:7–8, Luke 11:5–9, 18:1–8).

Repetitive Prayers

The term "repetitive prayer" may refer to a variety of things. Repetitive prayer may or may not be an issue, depending on "repetition."

Mantras

Repetitive prayer, in which a person repeats the same thing repeatedly, like a mantra or formula, is not scriptural. "And when you pray, do not load up meaningless phrases as the Gentiles do, because they imagine they will be heard for their numerous words," Jesus advises in Matthew 6:7. (ESV). The Greek term for "empty phrases" is also known as "vain repeats" or "babbling." It refers to repeating the exact phrases or a senseless, idle babble. It is not scriptural to "pray" merely by repeating a word or phrase repeatedly. Prayer is not a magical formula, spell, or desire to speak the "correct" words in the appropriate amount of time. Bead-counting is not prayer. Prayer connects with the God of the cosmos, which was made possible by Jesus Christ's sacrifice. Vain repetition lends more credibility to superstition than it does to God's work. It is not our prayers or the number of words we say that have power, but the God to whom we pray.

Habits or Routine

Praying the same thing again or providing prayers with identical phrasing may also be classified as "repetitive prayer." Some individuals, for example, like reciting the Lord's Prayer. Others have a predetermined prayer list. Or they just find themselves expressing the same things to God in prayer day after day, owing to natural comfort with specific wording and patterns of speech that come naturally to them. There is nothing inherently "wrong" with this style of prayer, but we should be mindful of our emotions. Is it really that we are praying, or are we just going through the motions?

An excellent approach to prayer is a discussion with a loved one. When our spouse asks how our day went, we usually say many of the same things daily. Repeating our phrases is not always a problem; it reflects the regular pattern of our days and discussions. However, when we merely react with "Good," we realise we have a communication failure. In our prayers, we may say the same thing. We may pray the same things repeatedly, even using the exact words. But if they're simply words, we've got a problem. We desire to connect with God rather than merely memorise words or talk by rote.

Remember that prayer is a gift. We have access to the Most High God. He is not an afterthought, and prayer is more than a routine. We desire to remain in a constant state of prayer (1 Thessalonians 5:17) and confidently approach God's throne of grace (Hebrews 4:16). But we also want to be confident that we are paying attention to the One who sits on the throne and not merely talking words for the sake of saying them.

Persistent Intercessions

Persistent prayer may be regarded as a sort of repetitious prayer in specific ways. We've all prayed for years for the salvation of a lost loved one, repairing a broken relationship, or forgiving a recurrent sin. Jesus urged us to keep going to God with our petitions in the parables of the needy neighbour (Luke 11:5–10) and the persistent widow (Luke 18:1–8). "We should constantly pray and never give up," says the Bible (Luke 18:1). Persistent prayer strengthens our reliance on God and reveals our understanding that only He can genuinely transform the situation. It is a method for us to be honest with God and regularly present the burdens on our hearts to Him. We are God's children in Christ, and He adores us. If an unfair judge answers merely because we continue to ask, how much more will our just Heavenly Father respond when we seek Him in prayer?

Vain Repetition

"When you pray, use not empty repetitions, as the heathen do: for they believe that they shall be heard for their much saying," Jesus stated in the Sermon on the Mount (Matthew 6:7, KJV). Because the term vain implies "empty" or "useless," Jesus reminds us that repeating meaningless sentences when we pray will not strengthen them to be heard by God. Our Father isn't bothered with word count, fancy language, or mantras; He seeks truth in our inner being (Psalm 51:6, ESV).

The King James Version of Matthew 6:7 says, "Use not vain repetitions." Other versions read, "Do not utilise meaningless repetition" (NASB), "Do not pile up empty sentences" (ESV), or "Do not continue rambling" (NIV). The use of repeated words or formulaic sentences, as Jesus points out, is a "heathen" or "pagan" practice that should not be used in Christian prayer. Our prayers should be more like Elijah's brief, uncomplicated prayer on Mt. Carmel and less like the prophets of Baal's extensive, repetitive petitions (see 1 Kings 18:25–39).

When we pray, we converse with God and honour Him. It's like a heartfelt chat. Many faiths, including certain sects of Christianity, have repetitive prayers that they recommend being said repeatedly. Some churches even compel members to say a particular prayer several times to forgive sin. Such formulaic prayers are vain repetitions that have no place in the church. They are a return to paganism and superstition. Jesus has already redressed our sins once and for all (Hebrews 10:10). We may approach the throne of grace with confidence based on Christ's sacrifice (Hebrews 4:15–16), not because of our floral, flattering words (Matthew 6:7).

It's easy to get caught up in pointless repetitions, repeating the exact phrases in our prayers rather than thinking about them or allowing them to emerge from the heart. In prayer, we should be focused on God and respect Him in our hearts. "These people draw close to me with their mouths and respect me with their lips," God declares in Isaiah 29:13, "but their hearts are distant from me."

Jesus' caution against meaningless repeats implies that we should avoid meaningless or vain phrases and repetition in our prayers. Repeating things wastes time but does not demonstrate our dedication or improve our chances of God hearing us. We should educate our children to pray naturally and conversationally concerning the One they are addressing from an early age.

Persisting in prayer is different to repeating yourself in vain. There is no harm in praying for the same item several times (see 2 Corinthians 12:8). After all, Jesus told us to "always pray and never give up" (Luke 18:1). However, it is acknowledged that our prayers are heartfelt, spontaneous, and respectful to God, rather than reciting words prepared by someone else.

The Bible instructs us to pray with confidence (James 1:6), directly to God (Matthew 6:9). In Jesus' name (John 14:13). Prayers should be offered with respect and humility (Luke 18:13), persistence (Luke 18:1), and surrender to God's plan (Matthew 6:10). The Bible instructs us to avoid insincere prayers intended merely for men's ears (Matthew 6:5) or depend on vain repetitions (Matthew 6:7).

Prayer and changing God's mind

To consider this puzzle, we divide it into two parts: 1) Does prayer influence God's decision? 2) Does prayer make a difference? The first question is answered negatively: God does not modify His mind. Yes, the response to the second question is that prayer does affect things. So, how can prayer affect change without affecting God's mind?

To begin with, for God to alter His mind, He would have to improve in some manner. In other words, if God altered His mind, it would imply that His first method of thinking was flawed, but since we prayed, He improved His plan for our predicament. We alter our minds when we see a better method to accomplish something. We first considered A but changed our minds after realising B was superior. However, God knows everything from beginning to finish (Revelation 22:13; Ephesians 1:4), so He cannot improve on any plan He has devised. His plans are already complete (2 Samuel 22:31), and He has indicated that His plans will be successful (Isaiah 46:9–11).

What about Exodus 32:14, which indicates that God "repented" of His actions? The Hebrew term "nacham", which is often translated as "repentance" or "change of heart," may also signify "sorrow" or "to provide consolation." This term first appears concerning the Lord in Genesis 6:6: "The LORD grieved that he had produced human beings on the earth, and his heart was much afflicted." This tends to imply that God reconsidered His choice to create humans. However, we must seek a different interpretation since God's methods are flawless. Using the secondary meanings of the word translated "regretted," we might interpret this phrase to suggest that man's evil caused God tremendous pain, particularly in light of what He must do to restore them.

Another use of the Hebrew term nacham is found in Jonah 3:10 (WEB):

God saw their works, that they turned from their evil way. God relented from the disaster, which he had said he would do to them, but he didn't do it.

In other words, God was relieved that He would not have to annihilate the Ninevites as He had promised. He didn't modify His decision since He already knew they'd repent. His activities are always part of a larger plan before creating the universe. "And if that country I warned repents of its iniquity, then I will relent and not inflict on it the tragedy I had prepared," Jeremiah 18:8 says. God is not altering His mind; instead, He takes solace in the fact that man's repentance will mitigate the penalties that He, in His righteousness, has already decreed.

So, why do we pray if it doesn't affect God's mind? Does prayer make a difference in our lives? Yes. God delights in transforming our circumstances in answer to our faith-filled petitions. "Always pray and do not lose heart," Jesus said (Luke 18:1). John 5:14–15 tells us that He listens and responds when we pray, following God's will. "According to His will" is the critical phrase. This will involve His time as well.

Consider this: a parent intends to buy his daughter a vehicle when she reaches the age of 16. He knows she'll have a job, be involved in church and school activities, and be able to pay for her own insurance by then. But he also intends to wait till she asks for it since he wants her to appreciate such a gift. However, at the age of 11, she asks for a vehicle. She begs, bargains, and becomes enraged when she is still without a vehicle on her 12th, 13th, and 14th birthdays. She grows and stops asking, but at 16, she approaches her father more carefully, explains her desire for a vehicle, and expresses her faith that her father would meet this need. He enthusiastically delivers her the keys in a matter of seconds. Was he persuaded to alter his mind? He had always intended to present it to her. Was it necessary for her to inquire? Yes, it was a factor in his choice.

Similarly, our heavenly Father asks us to ask Him for everything we need. When it is in His plan, He delights in giving it to us. He understands that we don't always understand His timetable, but He wants us to trust rather than mistrust (James 1:5–6; Matthew 6:8). Our prayers assist in aligning our hearts with His heart until His desire is our ultimate objective (Luke 22:42). When our hearts are entirely His, He pledges to listen and grant our wishes (Psalm 37:4; 2 Chronicles 16:9).

Unanswered Prayer

Many believe that answered prayer refers to God answering a prayer request. If a prayer request is denied, it is called an "unanswered" prayer. However, this is a misunderstanding of prayer. Every prayer that is raised to God gets answered. God sometimes responds with "no" or "wait." God only promises to answer our prayers if we ask, following His desire.

What exactly does it mean to pray following God's will? Praying according to God's will includes praying for things that honour and praise God and praying for what the Bible plainly shows to be God's will. God will not grant our request if we pray for anything that is not honourable to God or not under God's intention for our life. How can we determine God's will? When we pray for wisdom, God promises to provide it to us. "If any of you lacks knowledge," James 1:5 says, "he should seek God, who gives liberally to everyone without finding fault, and it will be given to him." 1 Thessalonians 5:12-24 is a fantastic place to start since it describes several aspects of God's desire for us. The more we grasp God's Word, the better we can pray (John 15:7). The more we know about what to pray for, the more we will often say "yes" to our petitions.

How many Believers have prayed for somebody only to have their prayers go unanswered? How many individuals have prayed and then given up because they became disappointed based on a lack of faith or determined that whatever they were asking for was not God's will? However, how we deal with unfulfilled prayer is essential not only for our own sake but also for the sake of others. We participate in the most essential and God-given dialogue with the One toward whom we must account for our problems when we pray. We were unquestionably bought at a high cost—the blood of the Lord Jesus Christ—and hence belong to God.

Our right to pray is given to us by God because it is as much ours now as it was when it was given to Israelites (Deuteronomy 4:7). However, there are times when we pray or speak to God, and He does not seem to reply. There might be many explanations for this. The Bible reveals why and how our prayers are answered by our attentive and loving God, who, as our representative, enjoys our spiritual connection with the Father (Hebrews 4:15).

Unconfessed sin is a primary reason why prayers go unanswered. God cannot be fooled or tricked, and He who sits enthroned above knows us intimately, even our most private thoughts (Psalm 139:1-4). If we do not live our faith, hold hostility against someone, or ask for things through the wrong motivation, we might anticipate God not to answer our request (2 Chronicles 7:14; Psalm 66:18; James 4:3). The potential advantages we gain from God's vast kindness are removed by our sin. Indeed, our petitions may be deemed terrible in God's eyes, especially when we manifestly do not belong to the Lord, through disbelief (Proverbs 15:8) or falseness (Mark 12:40).

Prayer may go unanswered because the Lord is extracting stronger dependence and confidence in Him from our faith, which should bring us a more profound feeling of thanks, love, and humility. As a result, we profit spiritually, for He grants grace to those who are humble (James 4:6; Proverbs 3:34). How does one feel for the poor Canaanite lady who begged our Lord for compassion when He was in Tyre and Sidon (Matthew 15:21-28). She was not a person a Jewish rabbi would be interested in. She was not Jewish; she was a woman, which would make any Jew ignore her. The Lord does not seem to respond to her requests, although He is well aware of her circumstances. He may not have responded instantly to her demands, but He listened and fulfilled her plea.

God may seem quiet to us sometimes, but He never sends us away empty-handed. Even if our prayers have not been answered, we must trust that God will do it in His time. Even if praying benefits us, we are moved to pray because of our faith. Faith is what pleases God (Hebrews 11:6), and if our prayer habit is lacking, does this not reflect our spiritual position as well? God hears our destitute calls for compassion, and His silence inspires us to persevere in prayer. He enjoys it when we try to reason with Him. Let us thirst for things close to God's heart and follow His ways rather than our own. If we are faithful to pray without stopping, we live in God's will, which can never be incorrect (1 Thessalonians 5:17-18).

Praying in Jesus' Name

In John 14:13-14 (WEB), it is said,

Whatever you ask in my name, I will do so that the Father may be glorified in the Son. If you will ask anything in my name, I will do it.

Some misinterpret this text, believing that stating "in Jesus' name" after a prayer guarantees God will always give what is requested. This amounts to treating the words "in Jesus' name" as a magic formula. This is entirely against the Bible.

Praying in Jesus' name entails praying with His power and requesting that God the Father act on our requests since we come in the name of His Son, Jesus. Praying in Jesus' name is equivalent to praying according to God's will:

This is the boldness which we have toward him, that, if we ask anything according to his will, he listens to us. And if we know that he listens to us, whatever we ask, we know that we have the petitions we have asked of him. (1 John 5:14-15 WEB).

When you pray in Jesus' name, you ask for things that will honour and glorify Jesus. After a prayer, the phrase "in Jesus' name" is not a secret formula. Saying "in Jesus' name" is pointless if what we ask for or say in prayer is not for God's glory and following His will. Praying in Jesus' name and for His glory is more vital than adding specific phrases after a prayer. The words in the prayer are not the most important, but rather the intention behind the prayer. The essence of praying in Jesus' name is to pray for things by God's will.

Prayer and faith

According to Hebrews 11:1, faith is "being certain of what we hope for and certain of what we do not see." Faith is perhaps the most crucial aspect of Christian existence. We cannot buy, sell, or gift it to our friends. So, what exactly is faith, and how does it play a part in the Christian life? Faith is defined by the dictionary as "believe in, loyalty to, or confidence in someone or something, particularly without rational evidence." Faith is also defined as "belief in and devotion to God." The Bible emphasises faith and how crucial it is. Indeed, faith is so crucial that we have no place with God without it and cannot satisfy Him (Hebrews 11:6). According to the Bible, faith believes in the one real God without seeing Him.

Where does faith come from? Faith is not something we create, nor is it something we are born with, nor is it the fruit of hard work in study or spiritual pursuit. Faith is a gift from God, not something we deserve, earn, or deserve to have, according to Ephesians 2:8-9. Faith comes from God. It is not achieved by our power or free will. God just gives us faith, along with His kindness and compassion, according to His divine plan and purpose, and He receives all the praise as a result.

Why have faith? God devised a method for distinguishing between people who belong to Him and those who do not, known as faith. Simply put, we need faith to satisfy God. God informs us that it pleases Him that we believe in Him despite our inability to see Him. According to Hebrews 11:6, "he blesses those who seek him sincerely." This is not to argue that we have confidence in God just to receive anything from Him.

On the other hand, God delights to reward loyal and faithful people. In Luke 7:50, we have an excellent illustration of this. When Jesus converses with a wicked woman, He offers us a peek at why faith is so beneficial. "You have been rescued by your faith; depart in peace." The lady had confidence in Jesus Christ, and He repaid her for it. Finally, faith keeps us going till the end, knowing that we shall be in paradise with God for all eternity if we believe. "Even though you haven't seen him, you love him; and even though you haven't seen him yet, you believe in him and are filled with an inexpressible and beautiful pleasure because you have received the objective of your faith, the salvation of your souls" (1 Peter 1:8-9).

Examples of faith. Hebrews chapter 11 (WEB) is regarded as the "faith chapter" because it describes remarkable acts of faith:

Faith is assurance of things hoped for, proof of things not seen. [2] For by this, the elders obtained testimony.

[3] By faith, we understand that the universe has been framed by the word of God so that what is seen has not been made out of visible things.

[4] By faith, Abel offered God a more excellent sacrifice than Cain, through which he had testimony given to him that he was righteous, God testifying concerning his gifts. Through it, he, being dead, still speaks.

[5] By faith, Enoch was taken away so that he wouldn't see death, and he was not found because God translated him. For he had had testimony given to him that before his translation, he had been well pleasing to God.

[6] Without faith, it is impossible to be well pleasing to him, for he who comes to God must believe that he exists and that he is a rewarder of those who seek him.

[7] By faith, Noah, being warned about things not yet seen, moved with godly fear and prepared a ship to save his house. Through this, he condemned the world and became the heir of righteousness according to faith.

[8] By faith, Abraham, when he was called, obeyed to go out to the place which he was to receive for an inheritance. He went out, not knowing where he went.

[9] By faith, he lived as an alien in the land of promise, as in a land not his own, dwelling in tents with Isaac and Jacob, the heirs with him of

the same promise. [10] He looked for the city with the foundations, whose builder and maker is God.

[11] By faith, even Sarah herself received power to conceive, and she bore a child when she was past age since she counted him faithful who had promised. [12] Therefore as many as the stars of the sky in multitude, and as innumerable as the sand which is by the sea shore, were fathered by one man, and him as good as dead. [13] These all died in faith, not having received the promises, but having seen them and embraced them from afar, and having confessed that they were strangers and pilgrims on the earth. [14] For those who say such things, make it clear that they are seeking their own country. [15] They would have had enough time to return if they had been thinking of that country from which they went out. [16] But now they desire a better country, that is, a heavenly one. Therefore, God is not ashamed of them, to be called their God, for he has prepared a city for them.

[17] By faith, Abraham, being tested, offered up Isaac. Yes, he who had gladly received the promises was offering up his one and only son, [18] to whom it was said, "Your offspring will be accounted as from Isaac," [19] concluding that God can raise up even from the dead. Figuratively speaking, he also did receive him back from the dead.

[20] By faith, Isaac blessed Jacob and Esau, even concerning things to come.

[21] By faith, Jacob, when he was dying, blessed each of the sons of Joseph and worshipped, leaning on the top of his staff.

[22] By faith, Joseph, when his end was near, made mention of the departure of the children of Israel and gave instructions concerning his bones.

23 *By faith, Moses, when he was born, was hidden for three months by his parents because they saw that he was a beautiful child and was not afraid of the king's commandment.*

24 *By faith, Moses, when he had grown up, refused to be called the son of Pharaoh's daughter, 25 choosing rather share ill-treatment with God's people than to enjoy the pleasures of sin for a time; 26 accounting the reproach of Christ greater riches than the treasures of Egypt; for he looked to the reward.*

27 *By faith, he left Egypt, not fearing the king's wrath, for he endured, as seeing him who is invisible.*

28 *By faith, he kept the Passover and the sprinkling of the blood so that the destroyer of the firstborn should not touch them.*

29 *By faith, they passed through the Red Sea on dry land. When the Egyptians tried to do so, they were swallowed up.*

30 *By faith, Jericho's walls fell after they had been encircled for seven days.*

31 *By faith, Rahab, the prostitute, didn't perish with those who were disobedient, having received the spies in peace.*

32 *What more shall I say? For the time would fail me if I told of Gideon, Barak, Samson, Jephthah, David, Samuel, and the prophets; 33 who, through faith subdued kingdoms, worked out righteousness, obtained promises, stopped the mouths of lions, 34 quenched the power of fire, escaped the edge of the sword, from weakness were made strong, grew mighty in war, and caused foreign armies to flee.*

35 *Women received their dead by resurrection. Others were tortured, not accepting their deliverance, that they might obtain a better resurrection.*

36 *Others were tried by mocking and scourging, yes, moreover by bonds and imprisonment.*

37 They were stoned. They were sawn apart. They were tempted. They were slain with the sword. They went around in sheep and goat skins, being destitute, afflicted, ill-treated 38 (of whom the world was not worthy), wandering in deserts, mountains, caves, and the holes of the earth.

39 These all, having had testimony given to them through their faith, didn't receive the promise,

40 God has provided some better things concerning us so that they should not be made perfect apart from us.

Behaviour demonstrates the presence of faith.

Faith is essential to Christianity. We have no place with God until we demonstrate confidence and trust in Him. By faith, we believe in God's existence. Most people have a hazy, jumbled idea of who God is but lack the respect required for His high position. These individuals lack the genuine faith to connect with the God who loves them. Our faith might waver at times, but since it is a gift from God, He gives moments of hardship and testing to confirm that our faith is genuine and hone and deepen it. This is why James advises us to consider it "pure pleasure" when we face difficulties, since testing our faith promotes persistence and maturity, proving that our faith is genuine (James 1:2-4).

Praying in the spirit

The phrase "praying in the Spirit" appears three times in the Bible. So what must I do? asks First Corinthians 14:15. I will pray with my spirit and mind and sing with my spirit and intellect. And pray in the Spirit on all circumstances with all sorts of petitions and requests, Ephesians 6:18 states. Continue to be attentive and pray for all the saints. But you, my friends, strengthen yourselves in your holy faith and pray in the Holy Spirit we read in Jude 20. So, what exactly does praying in the Spirit entail?

The Greek term "pray in" has multiple distinct meanings. It may indicate "by way of," "with the assistance of," "in the context of," and "with relation to." Praying in the Spirit is not about the words we use. Rather, it pertains to how we pray. Praying in the Spirit is praying in response to the Spirit's prompting. It is praying for things that the Holy Spirit prompts us to pray for. "In the same manner, the Spirit helps us in our weakness," says Romans 8:26. We have no idea what to pray for, but the Spirit Himself intercedes for us with sighs that words cannot describe."

Some people associate praying in the Spirit with praying in tongues, citing 1 Corinthians 14:15. Paul states, "pray with my spirit" while discussing the gift of languages. According to First Corinthians 14:14, when a person prays in tongues, he does not understand what he is saying since it is uttered in a language he does not understand. Furthermore, no one else can comprehend what is said (1 Corinthians 14:27-28). Paul teaches us in Ephesians 6:18 to "pray in the Spirit on all occasions with all sorts of petitions and requests." How can we pray for the saints with various pleas and requests if no one, even the one praying, knows what is being said? As a result, praying in the Spirit should be interpreted as praying in the Spirit's power, by the Spirit's leadership, and according to His will, rather than praying in tongues.

Prayers and Bible characters

Hannah

Hannah, one of Elkanah's two wives, resided "in the hill area of Ephraim" near Shiloh. Peninnah, Elkanah's second wife, had children, but Hannah did not. Hannah was devastated as a result of this. She urgently wanted a kid but was unable to conceive. To make things worse, Peninnah made fun of Hannah's barrenness. Although Elkanah adored Hannah and was exceedingly pleasant to her (1 Samuel 1:5, 8), Peninnah's cruelty, besides Hannah's natural sadness, was too much for her to handle. Hannah cried out to God about her predicament. If God gave her a son, she swore to commit him to God as a Nazirite (a man set aside to serve God; see Numbers 6:1-8).

Eli (the priest at the tabernacle) noticed Hannah praying intently and quietly and misunderstood her anguish for intoxication. He made an ill-advised remark to persuade her to stop drinking, and she corrected him. "I've been praying here out of immense agony and despair," she said (1 Samuel 1:16). "Go in peace, let the God of Israel grant your prayer that you have made to him," Eli responds after Hannah describes her situation. Hannah felt better after that; she had gotten God's promise.

Hannah's request was answered by the Lord. She gave birth to Samuel, whose name means "Asked of God." She followed her pledge to the Lord when the boy was old enough, bringing him to Eli and presenting him to the Lord to serve in the tabernacle. Eli and Hannah both worshipped God there. Then Hannah spoke a wonderful prayer, described in 1 Samuel 2:1-10.

God is shown as the One who helps the weak in Hannah's plea. Hannah and Peninnah symbolise bie world's weakness and power. The powerful often insult the weak, yet God listens and saves the Hannahs of the world. Hannah's prayer challenges the hubris of the proud, comparing their arrogant statements with God's tremendous and far-reaching wisdom. "The mighty's bows are shattered," she adds, "but the weak tie on strength" (verse 4). "My heart exults in the Lord; my strength is exalted in the Lord," she starts her prayer. Hannah realised that her power stemmed from God, not herself. She was not proud of her power but thrilled with God's capacity to strengthen the weak.

Hannah's storey exposes God's most profound thoughts. God does not disregard human longing. God Himself obviously put Hannah's yearning for a child in her heart. Her spouse attempts to console her, exasperatingly asking, "Am I not more to you than 10 sons?" He doesn't understand why she can't be happy with what she has, which is him! But Hannah's longing for a son was unquenchable. Peninnah insulted her, and Eli reprimanded her, but God heard her. God did not punish her for being dissatisfied. We know that spiritual satisfaction is a great benefit (1 Timothy 6:6). But it doesn't imply that our human aspirations – even those that make us sad when they go unfulfilled – are wicked in God's view. He knows how we feel. He understands that "hope postponed makes the heart ill" (Proverbs 13:12). And He asks us to offer Him our desires (Philippians 4:6).

Hannah's narrative demonstrates how God may utilise human frailty to achieve great things. Hannah's son, Samuel, grew up to be a renowned man of God — the last judge and prophet who anointed Israel's first two kings. But why was Hannah's narrative required? Why not begin with Samuel in the tabernacle or at the beginning of his judgeship? Why not just give birth to him to a God-fearing couple and send an angel to advise them to consecrate their boy to God? In a nutshell, why include Hannah's grief? Because Hannah's narrative glorifies God. Hannah's frailty, confidence in God as she turned to Him, the zeal of her desire, and her faithfulness in presenting Samuel to God as promised are all proof of God's activity in her life. Her tears were predestined to be a part of the wonderful tale of what God was accomplishing in the history of Israel.

Every individual has aspirations that cannot be satisfied and situations that bring sadness. Many times, we just do not comprehend these concepts. However, Hannah's life demonstrates that God understands our tale from beginning to finish, that everything has a reason, and that confidence in Him is never misplaced.

Elijah

1 Kings 18 contains the account of Elijah and the prophets of Baal. After Israel had been without rain for more than three years as a punishment for their idolatry, the prophet Elijah approached the cruel king, Ahab and challenged him to a spiritual battle. The king was to assemble every one of Israel and the 450 prophets of the false deity Baal and the 400 prophets of the false goddess Asherah to Mt. Carmel (verse 19).

How long will you waver between two opinions? Elijah asked the people of Israel on Mt. Carmel. If the Lord is God, obey him; if Baal is God, obey him" (1 Kings 18:21). At that moment, the populace remained undecided. The prophets of Baal were then challenged by Elijah to prepare a bull as a gift for their god—Elijah would do the same—with one condition: they could not kindle a fire on their altar. The genuine God would be the one who responded with fire from the sky (verses 22–25).

The people agreed that this was an excellent idea, and the prophets of Baal were the first to go. The pagan prophets screamed and danced around their altar from sunrise until midday, but Baal did not respond. "Shout louder!" Elijah started to insult them. ... He must be a deity! Maybe he's deep in contemplation, or maybe he's busy, or maybe he's travelling. Perhaps he is dozing and needs to be roused" (1 Kings 18:27).

As a result, the Baal prophets "shouted louder and sliced themselves with swords and spears, as was their tradition, until their blood gushed." After midday, they maintained their wild prophecy until the evening sacrifice" (1 Kings 18:28–29). Nothing occurred despite hours of work. "There was no reaction, no one replied, no one paid heed," the historian observes of Baal worship (verse 29).

Elijah was repairing the Lord's altar; he summoned the people to him. He built a ditch around the altar with twelve stones. He then put wood on the altar and placed the bull's chopped parts on it. Elijah then instructed the people to douse the altar with twelve big water jars. The flood washed away the sacrifice and the wood, filling the trench (1 Kings 18:30–35).

At the time of the evening offering, Elijah the prophet came near. He said, "Yahweh, the God of Abraham, of Isaac, and of Israel, let it be known today that you are God in Israel and that I am your servant, and that I have done all these things at your word. Hear me, Yahweh, hear me, that this people may know that you, Yahweh, are God and that you have turned their heart back again." (1 Kings 18:36–37 WEB).

Then God accomplished something that Baal could never do: the LORD's fire descended from heaven and burned the burnt sacrifice, the wood, the stones, and the dust, "and also lapped up the water in the trench" (verse 38). The people of Israel fell down and acknowledged the Lord as their God (verse 39).

Following God's mandate in Exodus 22:20, Elijah instructed the people to kill the prophets of Baal. Following this occurrence, the Lord ended the drought and provided rain to the area (1 Kings 18:45).

The fantastic fire incident from heaven was a response to Elijah's request. God was attempting to re-direct His people's attention back to Himself. He utilised a drought to gain their attention before performing a stunning miracle via His prophet right before their eyes. Nobody who observed the incident questioned that the Lord was God and Baal was a helpless imposter. The Israelites' repentance was quickly followed by God's supply of rain.

"The prayer of a virtuous person is strong and effective," James says (James 5:16). He offers Elijah's prayer life as an example: "Elijah was a human being, just as we are. He prayed sincerely that it would not rain, and it did not rain for three and a half years on the land. He prayed again, and the skies delivered rain, and the ground produced its crops" (James 5:17–18).

Praying for the dead

Praying for the deceased is not taught in the Bible. Our prayers have no effect on someone who has died. The fact is that one's eternal fate is sealed at the moment of death. Either he is rescued by faith in Christ and is in heaven, where he is resting and enjoying God's presence, or he is in pain in hell. This reality is vividly shown in the stories of the wealthy man and Lazarus, the beggar. This account was clearly used by Jesus to illustrate that the unjust are forever alienated from God after death. They remember their rejection of Christ, that they are in anguish, and that their state cannot be repaired (Luke 16:19-31).

People who have lost someone are often advised to pray for the deceased and their family. Of course, we should pray for people in mourning, but not for those who have died. No one should ever imagine that someone may be able to pray for him after he has died, resulting in some type of beneficial consequence. According to the Bible, mankind's everlasting condition is decided by our acts throughout our earthly existence.

The soul who sins shall die. The son shall not bear the father's iniquity, nor shall the father bear the son's iniquity. The righteousness of the righteous shall be on him, and the wickedness of the wicked shall be on him. (Ezekiel 18:20 WEB).

According to the writer of Hebrews, man is destined to die once and then face judgement (Hebrews 9:27). We see here that no improvement in a person's spiritual state can be accomplished after death, either by himself or via the efforts of others. If praying for the living, who are doing a sin that leads to death (1 John 5:16), i.e., continuing sin without seeking God's forgiveness, is pointless, how can praying for the dead serve them, given that there is no post-mortem plan of salvation?

We each have only one life, and we are accountable for how we live it. Others may affect our decisions, but we must ultimately answer for our decisions. There are no more options; we are forced to face judgment. Others' prayers may communicate their aspirations but will not influence the result. The time to pray for someone is while they are still alive, and the prospect of changing their heart, attitudes, and conduct exists (Romans 2:3-9).

It is normal to want to pray when we are in pain, suffering, or have lost loved ones or friends. Still, we also recognise the limits of acceptable prayer as the Bible teaches. The Bible is the only authentic prayer book, and it teaches that praying for the dead is pointless. Nonetheless, praying for the deceased is practised in certain sections of Christendom. For example, Roman Catholic theology allows prayers to the dead on their behalf. Even Catholic officials recognise that there is no express authorisation in the sixty-six books of canonical Scripture for prayers on behalf of the deceased. Instead, they use the Apocrypha (2 Maccabees 12:45), church tradition, the decision of the Council of Trent, and other sources to justify the practice.

According to the Bible, people who have surrendered to the will of the Savior (Hebrews 5:8-9) come directly and quickly before God after death (Luke 23:43; Philippians 1:23; 2 Corinthians 5:6, 8). So, what need do they have for the prayers of humans on Earth? While we grieve for those who have lost loved ones, we must remember that now is the time of God's favour; now is the day of salvation (2 Corinthians 6:2). While the context relates to the whole gospel era, the passage applies to anyone unprepared to face the inevitable—death and the judgement (Romans 5:12; 1 Corinthians 15:26; Hebrews 9:27). Death is irrevocable, and no amount of prayer can bring a person back to the salvation he rejected in life.

The Bible expressly forbids praying to the dead. According to Deuteronomy 18:11, anybody who consults with the dead is detestable to the Lord. Something to remember when consulting a medium.

The narrative of Saul contacting a medium to summon the ghost of a deceased person. Samuel was killed because he was disloyal to the

LORD; he did not obey the word of the LORD and even sought instruction from a medium (1 Samuel 28:1-25; 1 Chronicles 10:13-14). God has clearly said that such acts are not to be done.

Consider God's qualities. God is omnipresent (present everywhere simultaneously) and capable of hearing every global request (Psalm 139:7-12). A human person, on the other hand, lacks this quality. Furthermore, God is the only one who can answer prayer. God is omnipotent—he is all-powerful (Revelation 19:6). This is a trait that no human person, dead or living, has. Finally, God is omniscient, which means He knows everything (Psalm 147:4-5). Even before we pray, God knows and understands our actual needs better than we do. He not only knows what we need, but He also answers our petitions according to His perfect will.

So, for a dead person to accept prayers, the dead person must hear the petition, respond to it, and answer it in the most remarkable manner possible for the person praying. Only God hears and responds to prayer because of His flawless nature and what some theologians call His immanence. Immanence is a characteristic of God that allows Him to be intimately concerned with the concerns of humans (1 Timothy 6:14-15); this includes answering prayer.

Even when a person dies, God remains concerned about him and his fate. According to Hebrews 9:27, "...man is destined to die once, and then to face judgment." If a believer dies, he goes to heaven to be with the Lord (2 Corinthians 5:1-9, particularly verse 8); if a person dies in sin, he goes to hell, and everyone in hell will finally be cast into the lake of fire (Revelation 20:14-15).

God sent His Son, Jesus Christ, to be the intermediary between man and God (1 Timothy 2:5). We may approach God via Jesus Christ as our mediator. Why would we wish to journey through a wicked dead person, mainly when doing so risks incurring God's wrath?

Bibliography

Bounds, E. M. 1990. *The Complete Works of E. M. Bounds*. Grand Rapids: Baker.

Christenson, E. 1981. *What Happens When Women Pray*. Wheaton: Scripture Press, Victor Books.

Hallesby, O. 1975. *Prayer*. Minneapolis: Augsburg Publishing House.

Lawrence, B. 1975. *The Practice of the Presence of God*. Grand Rapids: Baker.

Murray, A. 1895. *With Christ in the School of Prayer*. Fleming H. Revell Co.

Storms, S. C. 1988. *Reaching God's Ear*. Wheaton: Tyndale.

Strauss, L. 1977. *Sense and Nonsense about Prayer*. Chicago: Moody Press.

White, J. 1977. *Daring to Draw Near*. Downers Grove: Inter-Varsity Press.

Wiersbe, W. 2010. *On Earth as it is in Heaven: How the Lord's Prayer Teaches Us to Pray More Effectively*. Baker Books.

About the Author

Andrew Lamont-Turner is a theological scholar, author, and Bible teacher who has dedicated his life to pursuing theological knowledge and disseminating spiritual wisdom. With a profound understanding of the scriptures and a passion for teaching, Andrew has emerged as a leading voice in the field of theology. His extensive academic qualifications and love for God and his family have shaped him into a multifaceted individual committed to nurturing spiritual growth and intellectual exploration.

Academic Journey: Andrew's academic journey reflects his thirst for theological understanding. He holds a Bachelor of Theology, Bachelor of Theology (Honours), Master of Theology, and a Doctor of Philosophy in Theology. These qualifications represent years of rigorous study and a commitment to excellence in his field. Furthermore, Andrew's intellectual curiosity extends beyond theology, as he also possesses a Bachelor of Education (Honours) and several Postgraduate Certificates in various commercial fields. This interdisciplinary approach has enriched his perspective and broadened his ability to connect theological principles with everyday life.

Teaching and Writing: Andrew's knowledge of theology has been expressed through his teaching and writing endeavours. As an educator, he has inspired countless students through his engaging lectures and insights into the scriptures. His ability to distil complex theological concepts into accessible teachings has garnered him a reputation as an exceptional communicator.

In addition to his teaching, Andrew is a prolific author who has published several books and a comprehensive Bible study series. His books delve into various aspects of Christian theology, offering insights, practical guidance, and thought-provoking reflections. With meticulous research, clear exposition, and a genuine desire to bridge the gap between academic theology and everyday faith, Andrew's writings have touched the lives of many, nurturing their spiritual growth and deepening their understanding of God's Word.

Pastoral Leadership: Living his faith ensures Andrew takes his Pastoral Leadership very seriously. He is the Pastor of a community church in rural South Africa, where he ensures the flock entrusted to him by God is well-fed and looked after.

Read more at https://ncts.education/nctseminary/course/view.php?id=25.

www.ingramcontent.com/pod-product-compliance
Lightning Source LLC
Chambersburg PA
CBHW051444140726
47987CB00006B/2529